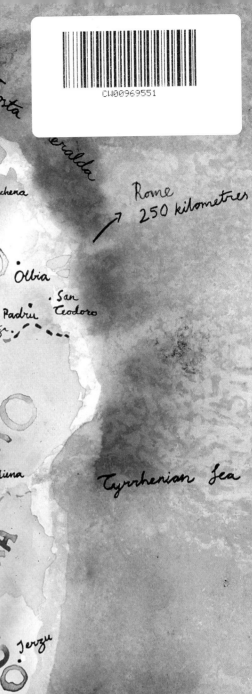

Strait of Bonifacio

Corta Smeralda

Rome
250 kilometres

GALLURA

OLBIA-
TEMPIO

• Azzachena

• Sennori

• Olbia

• Sassari

Tempio
Pausania

• San
Teodoro

SASSARI

• Oschiri

Padru
•

Sotza
•

• Alghero

Tyrrhenian Sea

• Bosa

NUORO

Nuoro
•

Oliena
•

ORISTANO

Caglieri •

OGLIASTRA

Oristano
•

Terzu
•

MEDIO
CAMPIDANO

CAGLIARI

• Sanjassi

CARBONIA-
IGLESIAS

• Serdiana

Carloforte
•

• Cagliari

SAN PIETRO
•

SANT'
ANTIOCO

Mediterranean Sea

This book is dedicated to my beautiful wife, Marilyn,
who is also my business partner and best friend –
and to my two amazing children, Martino and Sofia,
who inspire me and make me so proud every day.

Giovanni Pilu

This book is dedicated to my wonderful mother,
Joan Muir (1928–2011), whose love, strength, courage,
wisdom, love of life and example made it possible
for her daughter to live the life she dreamed of.

Roberta Muir

A SARDINIAN COOKBOOK

GIOVANNI PILU AND ROBERTA MUIR

PHOTOGRAPHY BY
ANSON SMART

jacqui small

INTRODUCTION

The rugged and untamed island of Sardinia has long been a place apart from mainland Italy, separated by language, culture and history, as well as geography. Here the rhythm of life is still largely determined by the seasons, with the year punctuated by the numerous festivals, or *feste*, held to celebrate local produce and successful harvests, as well as the major religious events of Christmas and Easter. Annual festivals for patron saints are another important part of the calendar and a great excuse for whole villages to come together to cook, eat, drink and enjoy each other's company.

Food, and the hospitality associated with sharing it, is integral to the Sardinian way of life. In Oliena, there's an annual event called *cortas apertas* ('the doors are open'), when local people open their homes to tourists and demonstrate the making of traditional foods. Following a way of life unchanged for centuries, the women still get up at 4 a.m. and make bread and bake sweets, and the men still milk the sheep then come home for breakfast before going to work (most of them have second jobs). Those who are too old to go to work or make the cheese that is considered essential at every meal, sell the milk – it's a little extra income that helps the family. Keeping a few cows or sheep is still common in Sardinia, even in non-farming households, and most homes have a vegetable garden. Before and after work people tend their garden and animals.

This was the Sardinia I grew up in. We always had a couple of cows, plus some chickens and rabbits – and although my father doesn't have any animals now, he's always had a vegetable garden. I have strong childhood memories of gathering berries, wild greens and herbs from the hedgerows on the way home from school, and of bringing down small birds with our sling shots. Long summer evenings would see us searching streams and creeks for trout and eels.

It was while I was studying to be a draftsman and working summer seasons in my uncle's bar that I realised what I wanted to do with my life, so I spent the next few years gaining some more experience in the kitchens of various resort hotels. Around this time, I met Marilyn Annecchini, who was born in Australia but whose family comes from the Italian region of Abruzzo. She was on a working holiday in Sardinia and we took a summer job together at a restaurant in San Teodoro, on the northeast coast. After the season finished she headed back to Australia . . . and not long after that, I followed.

Arriving in Sydney in 1992, I was full of enthusiasm and passion for the unique flavours of Sardinia. However, I spoke little English and, despite my hospitality experience, had no formal qualifications. We were living with Marilyn's parents in Terrey Hills at the time, and up the road was a restaurant called Il Piemonte, run by Piero Bignasca. He took me on in the kitchen, and that's where I started my apprenticeship, learning cooking and English side-by-side. Many years later when Piero wanted to retire, in a pleasing twist of fate, Lido Russo and I bought the restaurant from him and opened Cavallino, a casual place modelled on an Italian *agriturismo* (farm guesthouse).

A few years ago I went home for the festival of Saint Elias, the patron saint of the area where I grew up. The people of seven villages come together, many dressed in traditional costume, and carry the statue of the saint from the church down a long winding track to a field, where mass is celebrated outside under a huge tree.

The men cook whole sheep and cattle on a spit over an open fire and the women gather in the community hall to shred meat for a rich soup thats made in giant cauldrons. Families and friends set tables under trees and then the cauldrons of soup are carried around and served to all the guests.

Sheep's milk cheese and honey collected from wild hives are two of Sardinia's most distinctive ingredients, enriching an essentially rustic cuisine based on fruit, vegetables and grains.

In 1997, I opened my first restaurant, Cala Luna, in Mosman, Sydney, where I slowly introduced Sardinian specialities alongside more familiar Italian dishes. But it was with the opening of Pilu at Freshwater, Sydney, with Marilyn, in 2004, that I really drew on my Sardinian heritage to offer a menu of Sardinian food, including a tasting menu matched with Sardinian wines.

While there are some uniquely Sardinian ingredients, I firmly believe you can cook Sardinian food anywhere in the world using local produce; this is still regional cooking. There are some specific imported ingredients I use because they aren't available in Australia, but I also think it's essential to support local producers as much as possible. I used to import bottarga, the air-dried mullet roe that gives many Sardinian dishes their distinctive aroma and flavour (see page 93), but now I work with my Sardinian friend Massimo, who lives near Byron Bay, to produce our own; he also makes *salumi* from Berkshire rare-breed pork, including sausages flavoured with Sardinian Cannonau and Vernaccia wines. (For more information on finding and using Sardinian ingredients, see page 219.)

And when it comes to fruit and vegetables, imported produce may look perfect but often lacks flavour. I go to Sydney's fruit and vegetable wholesale market at Flemington every Tuesday morning, and my suppliers there know I don't want oranges from California or asparagus from Peru. Local farmers are struggling and I feel passionately about supporting them; if it's not in season, please cook something else and look forward to enjoying it when it is next in season.

I'm excited to be able to share with you the distinctive regional cooking of Sardinia, a place where dialects, traditions and cooking vary from one province – in fact, from one town – to the next. The dishes in this book are mostly from the province of Sassari, especially around my hometown of Sotza, in the region of Gallura. Throughout the book, I've given recipe titles in my dialect and in English, but people from other parts of Sardinia will often know the same dish by different names. But really, it doesn't matter what you call a dish. What matters is to cook it using the best seasonal produce you can find, and then to enjoy it with friends, family and good wine.

In Sardinia, almost any occasion offers a reason to eat and drink, and one of the things I miss most is casual weekend gatherings with friends. These usually involved plenty of good wine and high spirits, and we would often stay up late, feasting and drinking. I hope my recipes will encourage you to do the same with your friends and family, and to experience for yourself a taste of Sardinia.

Buon appetito!

Bread

Bread is an essential element of every meal in Sardinia – it's always on the table, often even between meals for a snack. When I first arrived in Australia, I couldn't believe that bread wasn't served at every meal; we'd be invited to friends' homes for dinner and I couldn't eat if there wasn't any bread on the table. Sardinia was considered a 'bread basket' for the Phoenicians and Romans because of the amount of grain it produced, so it's natural that bread has long been a staple of the Sardinian diet. Sardinian bread flour is called *farina salda* (which means 'Sardinian flour' in dialect): an unrefined flour, it's sometimes mixed with plain flour for making bread.

Apart from our famous flatbread, *pane carasau* (see page 6), there's *pasta dura* (literally 'hard dough'), a wood-fired bread with a hard, crisp crust. It's made in several shapes, including a *cornetto* (like a long croissant) and a small wheel. This is the bread I grew up with; breakfast was always *caffe latte* with this bread.

Most breads are made from wheat flour, but barley is sometimes used. Other ingredients that happen to be on hand, such as potato and the crisp bits of pork meat left over when lard is rendered down, are sometimes added for flavour and texture. *Panini all'olio* is made with quite a bit of olive oil: it's very moist and soft, and the crust is golden. The cheap rolls you buy from bakery chains resemble this in their softness, but miss out on colour and flavour. Round, flat breads called *cozzula* are popular and come in all sizes, from a snack-sized *panino* (bread roll) to huge wheels. When the dough is shaped into a diamond shape instead of a round, it becomes a *cogone* (or *coccone*, depending on your dialect).

The need to make bread light and durable enough for shepherds to take up into the hills, where they may stay for weeks at a time, led to a technique of double-baking, called *la biscottatura*, to produce thin, dry breads that are light to carry and won't go mouldy easily. *Pane carasau* is the most famous, but there are others, such as *pane pistoccu*, or Crisp Potato Bread (see page 8).

Of course food is never wasted in a peasant culture like Sardinia's, so there are many ingenious ways of using leftover bread. To this day, my sister, Alessandra, has *zuppa di latte* every evening before she goes to bed or while she's watching TV after dinner, breaking the leftover bread from the day into a coffee and adding two big spoonfuls of sugar (I prefer to add just a couple of biscuits for a touch of sweetness). Then there's one of my favourite dishes, *zuppa Gallurese*, which literally means 'soup from Gallura' but is more like a soufflé made from stale bread and mutton stock (see page 15).

In all its many shapes and sizes, bread will always be the first thing that appears on the Sardinian table, usually even before you sit down, and the last thing that will be taken away. It is as fundamental to our existence as water.

See also
- Stuffed Zucchini (page 49) in 'Vegetables'
- Veal-stuffed Eggplant (page 51) in 'Vegetables'
- Stuffed Artichokes (page 52) in 'Vegetables'
- Baked Mushrooms with Bread and Cured Pork Cheek (page 66) in 'Vegetables'

SARDINIAN FLATBREAD

PANE CARASAU

MAKES 24 PIECES

5 g fresh yeast or 2.5 g dried yeast
2 cups (500 ml) lukewarm water
1 kg bread flour, plus extra for dusting
1½ tablespoons fine sea salt

Bread making is part science, part art and part luck. The dough can be quite temperamental and affected by heat, humidity and draughts, and the greatest risk (and fear) is always that it won't rise. Although most people won't bother making this bread (in the photo on page 10) – which is very time consuming and is best baked in a wood-fired oven – even reading about the method is fascinating. I've adapted this recipe from one given to me by Francesca, a lady in my home village who learnt to bake from her mother and grandmother and still makes this bread every week. She uses the traditional fine linen cloths to cover the dough while it proves, starting with a roll of linen and folding the cloth over each disc as she adds it to the stack.

Mash the yeast into about 2 tablespoons of the water and stir until completely dissolved. Set aside in a warm place for about 20 minutes.

Sift the flour and salt into the bowl of an electric mixer fitted with a dough hook. With the machine running, pour in the yeast mixture and half the water and mix until absorbed. Then start adding remaining water a little at a time, to form a firm but pliable dough. You may not need it all; towards the end, it doesn't take much extra water for the dough to become too soft. Tip the dough onto a clean, lightly floured workbench and knead with the heels of your hands for about 5 minutes, until smooth and elastic.

Tear off a 100 g (tennis-ball sized) piece of dough and, holding it in two hands, repeatedly fold the sides under while turning the dough around, without stretching it out too much; the aim is to exclude as much air as possible while folding the dough into a smooth ball. Pinch the base of the ball closed, pinching off any excess dough and returning it to the remaining dough. Roll the ball between the palms of your hands to make it smooth, place on a lightly floured baking tray and cover lightly with plastic wrap and a clean tea towel. Repeat until all the dough is rolled into balls, placing them on the tray and keeping them covered as you go. Leave in a warm place for about 1 hour to rise slightly.

Test the dough by gently pressing the top of a ball with your finger: if the dough springs back into shape, it's ready; if your finger leaves an indentation, cover the dough and leave for another 30 minutes, then retest. The length of time needed will vary, depending on the temperature.

Using a rolling pin, roll out the first ball to form a 2 mm thick disc, place on a clean tea towel that's been lightly dusted with flour, dust the top of the disc lightly with flour and cover with another flour-dusted tea towel. Repeat with remaining balls, stacking the discs on top of one another with a clean, flour-dusted tea towel in between. Set aside in a warm place for about 1 hour to prove; in colder weather, this may take longer. Unfortunately there's no way to tell when the discs have proven sufficiently until you put the first one in the oven.

Meanwhile, preheat oven to its maximum temperature with an unglazed 30 cm × 30 cm terracotta tile (pizza brick) on the middle shelf (remove any shelf above the middle shelf).

Carefully turn the stack of tea towels and discs upside down, so that the disc you rolled first is now on the top. Open the oven door and slide the middle shelf out a little. Remove the top tea towel, then pick up the next tea towel with the first disc of dough on it. Using the tea towel to help you handle the dough, slide it onto the terracotta tile, gently easing it off the tea towel as you do so. Close the oven and watch the dough closely. Within a minute, it should puff up; if it doesn't, the dough hasn't proved for long enough, so return the stack of remaining discs to a warm place for a further 30 minutes.

Using an egg lifter or fish slice, remove the puffed disc of bread from the oven and place it on a cutting board (at this stage it should look like Lebanese bread or pita). Using a serrated knife, split the disc around the centre and peel it apart to give two discs. It may stick in places, in which case tear off whatever sections you can; torn bread tastes just as good! Turn the top half over and place it on top of the bottom half. Place a chopping board on top to weight it down. Repeat with the remaining discs, stacking the split discs (and any torn sections) on top of one another under the chopping board.

When all the discs have been part-baked and split, flip the pile over and place the top piece of bread back in the oven on the terracotta tile, keeping the chopping board on top of the remaining pieces. Cook for 1–2 minute, until it turns pale golden. Remove from oven, place on a clean, dry workbench and place a chopping board on top to prevent it curling. Repeat with remaining pieces, adding each cooked piece to the stack under the chopping board. Store in an airtight container for up to 3 months.

To serve as *pane guttiau* ('drizzled bread'), drizzle with olive oil, scatter with rosemary or thyme and salt flakes and warm in a preheated 160°C oven for about 10 minutes.

PANE CARASAU

Pane carasau is a thin, crisp, double-baked bread unique to Sardinia. It originated in the province of Nuoro in the centre of the island but has since spread widely. Traditionally, a large disc of dough is baked in a very hot wood-fired oven until it puffs up, then it's split in half and the two halves are returned to the oven to crisp. Even large modern bakeries still split the bread by hand – everything else (kneading, rolling and baking) can be mechanised, but the splitting has to be done by hand.

This bread, which is on the table almost everywhere you go in Sardinia, is usually made by bakers these days, though some people still cook it in their own wood-fired ovens at home (I've included a recipe on page 4, if you want to give it a go; see page 219 for details of where to buy *pane carasau*). It has become better known by its Italian name, *carta di musica* ('sheet music'), because it's like the fine parchment paper originally used to write music on. *Carasau* means to crisp up or toast, which is what happens when you split the bread and put it back into the oven. In my dialect it's called *pane fresa*, which has a slightly more obscure origin. When you work the land, first you till the soil with a plough, then you break up the soil by dragging a big spike-studded frame over it. This second tilling is called *fresare*, and because the bread is taken out into the fields to eat while this is being done, it's given the name *pane fresa*.

Pane carasau was made to be light and durable, so that it could easily be carried and stored for long periods of time – this meant that shepherds, who often lived in the hills with their flocks, with only very basic cooking facilities, could still have their essential bread with every meal. It can be eaten on its own, but is often used as a base for other dishes, sometimes rehydrated in a little stock or water then stacked with sauce and pecorino (see page 12). *Pane dolce* ('sweet bread') is *pane carasau* dipped in a thin batter of milk, eggs and flour and deep-fried then served drizzled with honey as a sweet treat alongside a cup of coffee. Most commonly it's served as *pane guttiau* ('drizzled bread'), drizzled with olive oil and scattered with rosemary (or thyme) and salt flakes, then warmed and crisped in the oven for a few minutes. It's what we offer to start every meal at my restaurant.

SOFT POTATO BREAD

COZZULA MUDDIZZOSA

MAKES ABOUT 16 PIECES

500 g desiree potatoes
fine sea salt
500 g bread flour, plus extra for dusting
20 g fresh yeast *or* 10 g dried yeast

Cozzula **is my dialect's word for round, flat bread, and** *muddizzosa* **means soft, almost puffy or downy like a comfortable pillow. When I was growing up we used to buy larger versions of this bread from the baker. About 20 cm wide and about 3 cm thick, they would be already cut in half and filled with mortadella and fontina, and one was enough for two people to share. These are mini versions (in the photo on page 10), perfect to serve with soups or for mopping up a rich ragù, as well as for sandwiches.**

Cook potatoes, in their skins, in boiling salted water for about 30 minutes, until a wooden skewer can be inserted without any resistance.

Meanwhile, mash the yeast into about 2 tablespoons of lukewarm water and stir until completely dissolved. Set aside in a warm place for about 20 minutes.

Sift flour and 1 teaspoon of salt into the bowl of an electric mixer fitted with a dough hook. Drain cooked potatoes well and pass through a potato ricer or coarse sieve into the bowl with the flour, then mix until roughly combined. Add yeast mixture and mix to form a firm dough. Tip the dough onto a clean, lightly floured workbench and knead with the heels of your hands for about 5 minutes, until smooth and pliable.

Tear off a 50 g (golfball-sized) piece of dough and roll into a ball, then place on a clean, lightly floured workbench and cover lightly with plastic wrap. Continue rolling balls of the dough, placing each one under the plastic wrap as you make it, to prevent it from drying out.

Using a rolling pin, roll all the balls into 1 cm thick discs. As you roll each disc, place it on a lightly floured perforated baking tray and cover with plastic wrap then a clean tea towel.

Leave in a warm place for about 2 hours to rise. Test by gently pressing the top of a ball with your finger: if it springs back into shape, it's ready; if it leaves an indentation, cover and leave for another 30 minutes, then retest. The length of time needed will vary, depending on the temperature.

Meanwhile, preheat oven to 170°C.

Place trays in oven and cook for 10 minutes, then swap the positions of the trays and cook for a further 5–10 minutes until well browned. Remove from oven and wrap in a clean tea towel until cool.

Note

Perforated trays for baking bread (so that the dough is heated from the top and the bottom) are available from specialty kitchenware stores and chefs' suppliers.

CRISP POTATO BREAD

PANE PISTOCCU

Pistoccu is an onomatopoeic word referring to the crunchiness of this flat, crisp bread with a crumbly texture similar to cornbread; it's a dialect word from Nuoro, the largest town in the Sardinian province of the same name. *Pane pistoccu* (in the photo on page 10) is made in a similar way to *pane carasau*: baked, then split and returned to the oven to dry out. This second baking, *la biscottatura*, was a popular way of preserving bread so that it could be taken up into the mountains or stored for long periods; *biscotti* (literally 'twice cooked') are made in a similar way. Stored in an airtight container in a cool, dry place, *pane pistoccu* keeps for months, so make a big batch that's worth the effort; it's great served as *assaggini* (nibbles with drinks, literally 'little tastes') with *salumi*, olives and cheese.

MAKES ABOUT 12 PIECES

250 g desiree potatoes
fine sea salt
15 g fresh yeast *or* 7.5 g dried yeast
350 ml lukewarm water
1 kg bread flour, plus extra for dusting

Cook potatoes, in their skins, in boiling salted water for about 30 minutes, until a wooden skewer can be inserted without any resistance.

Meanwhile, mash the yeast into about 2 tablespoons of the water and stir until completely dissolved. Set aside in a warm place for about 20 minutes.

Sift flour and 1 teaspoon of salt into the bowl of an electric mixer fitted with a dough hook. Drain cooked potatoes well and pass through a potato ricer or coarse sieve into the mixer bowl. With the machine running, pour in the yeast mixture and half the water and mix until absorbed. Start adding remaining water a little at a time, just until a firm but pliable dough forms. You may not need all the water; towards the end, it doesn't take much extra water for the dough to become too soft.

Tip the dough out onto a clean, lightly floured workbench and knead with the heels of your hands for about 5 minutes, until smooth. Transfer the dough to a flour-dusted bowl, place a clean, damp tea towel on the surface of the dough and set aside in a warm place for about 1 hour until dough has risen slightly and springs back when pressed; in colder weather, it may take longer.

Tear off a 200 g (grapefruit-sized) piece of dough and, on a clean, lightly floured workbench, roll out into a 4 mm thick rectangle. Place on a clean tea towel that's been lightly dusted with flour, dust the top of the dough with flour and cover with another flour-dusted tea towel. Repeat with remaining dough, stacking the rectangles on top of each other with a clean, flour-dusted tea towel between each one. Leave in a warm place for about 2 hours to rise. Test by gently pressing the top rectangle with your finger: if it springs back into shape, it's ready; if it leaves an indentation, cover and leave for another 30 minutes, then retest.

Meanwhile, preheat oven to its maximum temperature with an unglazed 30 cm × 30 cm terracotta tile (pizza brick) on the middle shelf (remove any shelf above the middle shelf).

Carefully turn the stack of tea towels and dough rectangles upside down, so that the rectangle you rolled first is now on the top.

Open the oven door and slide the middle shelf out a little. Remove the top tea towel, then pick up the next tea towel up with the first rectangle of dough on it. Using the tea towel to help handle the dough, slide it onto the terracotta tile, gently easing it off the tea towel as you do so. Close the oven and watch the dough closely. Within 2 minutes it should puff up.

Using an egg lifter or fish slice, remove the bread from the oven and place it on a cutting board (at this stage it should look like Lebanese bread or pita). Using a serrated knife, split the puffed bread into two layers, then turn the top half over and place it on top of the bottom half. Place a chopping board on top to weight it down. Repeat with remaining rectangles of dough, stacking the split bread under the chopping board.

Flip the pile of split bread over and place the top piece of bread back in the oven on the terracotta tile, cut side up, keeping the chopping board on top of the remaining pieces. Cook for 1–2 minutes, until it turns pale golden. Remove from oven and place on a clean, dry workbench. Repeat with remaining pieces of bread.

SARDINIAN SPICED NUT BREAD

PANI 'E SABA

MAKES 5 PIECES

40 g fresh yeast in one piece
　　or 20 g dried yeast
500 g tipo 00 flour, plus extra for dusting
60 g blanched almonds, roughly chopped
60 g shelled walnuts, roughly chopped
60 g pine nuts, roughly chopped
pinch of ground cloves
350 ml saba (see page 221)

This bread (in the photo on page 206) is popular served with cheese or for breakfast with ricotta; the name literally means 'bread and saba'. In some areas it's shaped into a ring and, after it's baked, it's dipped in hot saba and sprinkled with hundreds and thousands.

If using fresh yeast, soak the whole piece in ½ cup (125 ml) of warm water for a few minutes. If using dried yeast, stir it into just enough warm water to moisten – about 1–2 tablespoons.

Meanwhile, sift flour into the bowl of an electric mixer fitted with a dough hook, then add almonds, walnuts, pine nuts and cloves. With the machine running, drizzle in 250 ml of the saba and mix until combined.

If using fresh yeast, remove it from the water. Add fresh yeast, or dissolved dried yeast, to the dough and mix until well combined. Scrape down the sides of the bowl, then start adding remaining saba, a little at a time, to form a soft dough. You may not need it all; towards the end, it doesn't take much extra liquid for the dough to become too soft.

Tip dough onto a lightly floured workbench, dust lightly with flour and knead for a few minutes until dough is elastic, then roll into a log and cut into 5 pieces. Roll each piece into a ball, flatten slightly and place on a baking-paper-lined baking tray, spaced well apart. Cover loosely with plastic wrap then a tea towel and set aside in a warm place for about 5 hours to rise (as the dough is quite heavy, it may only rise a little – it's ready if it springs back when pressed).

Preheat oven to 170°C. Remove tea towel and plastic wrap from dough and place baking tray in oven. Cook the bread for 30 minutes, then test by inserting a wooden skewer: if it comes out dry, the bread is ready; if there is dough clinging to the skewer, return the bread to the oven for a further 5 minutes, then test again. Remove bread from oven and place on a wire rack to cool. Slice and serve.

PORK SCRATCHINGS BREAD

COGONE DE ELDA

MAKES ABOUT 28 PIECES

20 g fresh yeast *or* 10 g dried yeast
450 ml lukewarm water
1 kg bread flour, plus extra for dusting
1 teaspoon fine sea salt
160 g pork scratchings

Notes

To make 160 g pork scratchings: buy 400 g lardo (see page 220) and cut it into dice. Place in a frying pan over low heat until completely melted, then cook over medium heat for 10 minutes or so, until the solid bits are crunchy. Strain off the liquid fat – when cool, this can be used instead of butter to make various pastries (see pages 174, 183 and 202) – then drain the scratchings on paper towel. The pork scratchings can be stored for up to a week in an airtight container in a cool, dry place (do not refrigerate).

Perforated trays for baking bread (so that the dough is heated from the top and the bottom) are available from specialty kitchenware stores and chefs' suppliers.

Clockwise from left: Sardinian Flatbread (page 4); Crisp Potato Bread (page 8); Soft Potato Bread (page 7); Pork Scratchings Bread (this page)

Traditionally pork fat was melted down and used for everything: deep-frying, some pastry doughs, and to polish leather boots before hunting to waterproof them (which made them stink!). The bits of pork meat left behind when the fat was rendered were too good to waste and so were used to add flavour to this simple bread. My Zia (Aunt) Giovanna gave me this recipe and I adapted it for the restaurant. In winter I remember her covering the dough with blankets to keep it warm while it proved, and then wrapping the cooked bread in bed sheets after it came out of the oven so it wouldn't form a crisp crust. Because of the pork scratchings, these *cogone* are very tasty on their own, but they also make great sandwiches – mortadella is one of my favourite fillings. You can form the bread dough into rounds instead of diamond shapes, to make *Cozzula de Elda*.

Mash the yeast into about 2 tablespoons of the water and stir until completely dissolved. Set aside in a warm place for about 20 minutes.

Sift flour and salt into the bowl of an electric mixer fitted with a dough hook. With the machine running, add half the remaining water and mix until absorbed. Then start adding the remaining water a little at a time, just until the mixture begins to come together into a dry dough. Mix in yeast mixture and pork scratchings, adding a little more water if necessary to form a firm dough. You may not need all the water; towards the end, it doesn't take much extra water for the dough to become too soft. Tip the dough onto a clean, lightly floured workbench and knead with the heels of your hands for about 5 minutes, until smooth.

Cut the dough into 4 pieces. Roll the first piece into a thin log about 30 cm long. Dust workbench with a little more flour and, using a rolling pin, roll out into a rectangle about 1 cm thick. Starting from one corner, slice the rectangle on the diagonal into 5 cm wide strips to make diamond shapes. Add the off-cuts to the next piece of dough and repeat the rolling and slicing. Continue until all the dough is rolled and sliced into diamonds.

Dust 2 perforated baking trays lightly with flour. Place the strips of dough on the trays with a little space between them. Cover lightly with plastic wrap then clean tea towels and leave in a warm place for about 1½ hours to rise. Test by gently pressing the top of a strip with your finger: if it springs back into shape, it's ready; if it leaves an indentation, cover and leave for another 30 minutes, then retest. The length of time needed will vary, depending on the temperature.

Meanwhile, preheat oven to 170°C.

Place trays in oven and cook for 10 minutes, then swap the positions of the trays and cook for a further 10–15 minutes, until lightly browned. Remove from oven and wrap in a clean tea towel until cool.

FLATBREAD STACK WITH TOMATO SAUCE AND POACHED EGGS

PANE FRATTAU

SERVES 4

3 cups (750 ml) Passata (see page 218)
1 litre Mutton Stock (see page 215)
1 teaspoon salt flakes
4 eggs
8 sheets pane carasau (see page 6)
2 tablespoons finely sliced basil leaves
150 g aged Pecorino Sardo, freshly grated
extra virgin olive oil, for drizzling

This delicious dish using *pane carasau* is a quick, substantial one-dish meal for hungry shepherds or farmworkers. Typically, they would go out early in the morning and come back about 9.30 a.m. for a hearty breakfast that went into the centre of the table for everyone to share. I remember going hunting, leaving at 4.30 a.m. after just a coffee and a grappa, then stopping a couple of hours later for a big breakfast like this – followed by a late lunch after the hunting. In a couple of towns they use a *sugo di carne* (a ragù) instead of the passata to create a richer dish, and I like to add a little basil or parsley. (If your bunch of basil has any flowers, keep them to sprinkle over the *pane frattau* as a garnish.) I think this makes a great brunch dish.

Place passata in a saucepan and bring to a simmer. Keep warm over low heat.

Combine stock and salt in a small saucepan and bring to a simmer. Crack an egg into a cup and carefully slide it into the simmering stock. Repeat with a second egg. Cook eggs for 3 minutes then remove, using a slotted spoon, and place on paper towel to drain. Repeat with the remaining eggs.

Transfer stock to a large, tall saucepan over low heat. Using tongs, dip a sheet of pane carasau in and out of the hot stock to just soften it. Place on a platter and spread about 4 tablespoons of the passata over the top. Scatter about 1 teaspoon of the basil and 3 tablespoons of the pecorino on top of this. Dip another sheet of pane carasau in the hot stock, place it on top of the pecorino, top with more passata, basil and pecorino and continue the layering, finishing with a final layer of pecorino and a scattering of basil.

Cut the stack into quarters, top each quarter with a poached egg, then place on plates. Drizzle with olive oil and serve.

Notes

When you drop the egg into the stock to poach it, the weight of the yolk pulls it down and the lighter white wraps up around the yolk enclosing it – in Italian this is called *in camicia* ('in a shirt').

When you're softening the bread, don't worry if some of the sheets break – just reassemble them in the stack.

GALLURESE-STYLE BREAD PUDDING

ZUPPA GALLURESE

SERVES 6 AS A FIRST COURSE

200 g young Pecorino Sardo,
	freshly grated
handful mint leaves, finely sliced
1.2 litres Mutton Stock (see page 215)
salt flakes, to taste
1 loaf stale wood-fired bread,
	cut into 2 cm thick slices
8 large thin slices young provolone

Notes

Use sourdough or another bread with a dense crumb and a thick crust for this dish – it needs to be a few days old, to ensure it's quite dry and will soak up lots of stock; stale panini can also be used.

It's important to use a very young provolone with a mild flavour, rather than an aged cheese, and the slices need to be quite large so that four of them cover the entire dish (if the slices seem small, buy some extra).

This dish can also be made in four individual 500 ml ramekins or copper saucepans, as we do at the restaurant – in which case, it will only need to cook for about 30 minutes.

This dish is essentially a way to use up stale bread and leftover broth from a traditional dish of boiled mutton (see page 120). In peasant cuisines, such as Sardinia's, nothing is wasted and we use whatever's on hand: mint is in every Sardinian garden (it's a pest there – once you plant it, you can never get rid of it) and there's always pecorino in the pantry.

Although this is called a 'soup', the bread soaks up all of the stock and the end result is almost soufflé-like. This dish varies across Gallura, Sardinia's northernmost region: sometimes it's made with parsley, sometimes without, I've seen the stock made with a combination of beef, chicken and mutton, sometimes with just beef and, most commonly, with just mutton. Every cook has their own 'rules'. I once cooked this dish for a TV documentary filmed in a winery, and the lady there insisted my *zuppa Gallurese* wasn't authentic because I hadn't used tomatoes to give the stock a rich red colour, but my mother and aunties never use tomatoes in their versions.

Suppa cuata ('hidden soup') is a dialect name for this dish, since it was traditionally made by shepherds in a camp oven over an open fire – hot coals would be piled on top to give all-round heat, effectively 'hiding' the pot.

Preheat oven to 180°C.

Combine pecorino and mint.

Heat stock in a small saucepan and add salt.

Arrange a layer of bread in a 2-litre baking dish. Pour stock over it until the bread is soaked. Prick the bread with a fork and leave it for a few minutes to soak up all the stock, adding more stock until the bread won't absorb anymore.

Sprinkle half the pecorino and mint mixture over the top, packing it into any spaces between the bread slices, and cover with a layer of provolone. Add another layer of bread, tearing a slice into pieces if need be to fill any gaps. Soak with stock as above, pricking the bread with a fork before letting it sit for 5–10 minutes for the stock to soak in. Add a little more stock if it will take it – the bread should be saturated without too much extra stock sitting on the top or in the bottom of the dish (you may not need to use all the stock). Scatter the remaining pecorino mixture over the top, then cover with a layer of provolone.

Place in oven and cook for about 1 hour, until provolone is crusty and golden.
Set aside to rest for at least 20 minutes (it will sink in the centre as it settles).
Serve in the middle of the table, for people to help themselves.

Pasta
and Rice

Sardinia grows a lot of durum wheat, which is perfect for making dried pasta, so it's not surprising that pasta features strongly in the Sardinian diet. What may be surprising, though, is the wide variety of distinctive pasta shapes: the most popular is the shell-shaped *malloreddus*; then there are fat little *ciciones*, a type of gnocchi made with semolina flour; *lombrichi*, literally 'little worms'; chewy, coin-shaped *talluzzas*; and *maccarrones de busa*, rolled along a knitting needle or steel rod. Fregola, toasted semolina pasta (see page 106), is a legacy of the Arabic and North African influence on Sardinian food. In Sardinia, the name *culurzones* (also called *gulurjones*, *culingiones* or *culurgiones*, depending on the dialect) often refers to any filled pasta. Those made with the traditional filling of potato, cheese and mint, and distinctively shaped like an ear of wheat, are however unique to Sardinia. Rice dishes are also popular, as is couscous in some areas (mainly the south of the island, where the Arabic influence is strongest).

On an Italian menu, pasta is always a first course, never a main. Different types of pasta dough are used for different purposes: pasta served with meat sauces is made from a dough that doesn't contain egg, while filled pastas are made with a slightly softer, egg-rich dough.

Fresh pasta should always be cooked until it's tender; al dente refers only to dried pasta. Dried pasta manufacturers have their cooking times well tested, but I find the pasta often ends up a little beyond al dente by the time it's served. I suggest you cook it for 2 minutes less than the time given on the packet, as it will finish cooking in the sauce. Rustic pastas, like *malloreddus* and *ciciones*, take a long time to cook; when you eat them they'll still be chewy and not as tender as long pasta, but they're meant to be more doughy and substantial. (See page 222 for more tips on cooking pasta.)

The pasta, not the sauce, is the star of the dish. Good pasta sauces contain only a few ingredients and you mustn't drown the pasta in sauce; you should always be able to taste the pasta itself – that's why I love pasta *cacio e pepe*, with just pecorino and pepper. When I visited Italian artisanal pasta manufacturer Giovanni Fabbri, he made me taste his pasta three times before it was even sauced: first raw; then cooked; then tossed in just a little oil; and, finally, with the sauce. Toss the pasta with just enough sauce to coat it. Don't pour the sauce over the pasta – the exception is filled pasta, where you put the pasta on the plate and spoon the sauce over the top, so as not to break up the delicate parcels. Serve any excess sauce at the table in a separate bowl, so those who like their pasta extra saucy can add a little more. Many pastas are finished with a little butter or oil tossed through the sauce at the end (what Italians call *mantecare*), which gives a creamy result, as does adding a little of the pasta cooking water. The butter should be firm – not hard straight from the fridge, but certainly not starting to melt. When I was a young chef, I was told that you have to toss the pasta with the sauce at least ten times to allow the pasta to release some starch and give the sauce a creamy consistency.

See also
- Blue Mussel and Fregola Soup (page 100) in 'Seafood'
- Squid filled with Fregola, Olives and Pine Nuts (page 103) in 'Seafood'
- Prawns with Tomato, Chilli and Fregolone (page 106) in 'Seafood'
- Fregola and Olive Salad (Lamb Rump with Fregola and Olive Salad; page 116) in 'Meat and Poultry'
- Stracci Pasta with Braised Rabbit Sauce and Chestnuts (page 150) in 'Hunting and Foraging'
- Tonnarelli Pasta with Smoked Eel and Squid (page 161) in 'Hunting and Foraging'
- Nettle Tagliolini with Pecorino, Black Pepper and Cured Pork Cheek (page 162) in 'Hunting and Foraging'

MALLOREDDUS WITH CLAMS, BOTTARGA AND ZUCCHINI FLOWERS

MALLOREDDUS CON VONGOLE, BOTTARGA E FIORI DI ZUCCHINE

SERVES 4 AS A FIRST COURSE

½ quantity Fresh Pasta Dough #3 (see page 217), not rolled through pasta machine *or* 300 g dried malloreddus

6 female zucchini (courgette) flowers, with baby zucchini attached

fine sea salt, for pasta water

½ cup (125 ml) extra virgin olive oil

2 cloves garlic, finely sliced

1 small red chilli, finely chopped

1 kg vongole (clams), purged (see page 221)

30 ml Vermentino (see page 219) or other dry white wine

50 g bottarga (see page 93), freshly grated, sifted

2 tablespoons finely sliced flat-leaf parsley leaves

This isn't the traditional way of serving malloreddus (which are normally eaten with pork sausage sauce; see page 23), but it's one that I've developed for the restaurant – and it happens to be Roberta's favourite dish. Sometimes I add cherry tomatoes as well.

If making malloreddus, divide pasta dough into 3 pieces. Place one piece on a clean, dry workbench and, using the palms of your hands, roll into a sausage shape about 5 mm thick. Repeat with the remaining 2 pieces of dough. Cut the pasta 'sausages' into 1 cm lengths. Using a little pressure from your thumb, roll each piece of dough along a gnocchi board or clean, dry workbench to fold the dough into a closed shell shape.

Remove baby zucchini from the flower, trim off the end, then slice zucchini thinly. Remove and discard stamen from inside the flowers and tear off each petal.

Bring a large saucepan of water to the boil, add fine sea salt, then malloreddus and boil for about 8 minutes from the time the water returns to the boil (or according to packet instructions for dried malloreddus), until tender.

Meanwhile, heat a large frying pan, add ⅓ cup (80 ml) of the oil and, when hot, add garlic, sliced baby zucchini and chilli. Cook over medium heat for about 1 minute, then add vongole and wine. Cover, shake pan well and cook for another minute or two, until vongole open. Remove from heat and pick out any vongole that haven't opened. Using a blunt knife such as a butter knife, gently prise them open: if the meat is plump and intact on one side of the shell, use them; otherwise discard. Next, remove meat from half the shells and return to the pan. Add half the bottarga and cook for another minute.

When malloreddus are ready, drain well, reserving some of the cooking water. Add malloreddus to the sauce and toss for a minute or two to coat well, then stir in a couple of tablespoons of reserved cooking water, adding a little more if necessary to give a creamy consistency. Toss through the zucchini flower petals and remaining oil. Sprinkle with parsley and remaining bottarga, then serve immediately.

Malloreddus

Malloreddus, along with fregola (see page 106) is Sardinia's most distinctive pasta. It's a heavy gnocchi-style pasta, like small shell-shaped dumplings with a rough outer surface and a smooth inner surface. These are also known by different dialect names, including *maccarrones caidos* and *maccarrones cravaos*, and there's a type made with barley called *maccarrones de orgiu* (*orgiu* being dialect for *orzo*, the Italian for barley). *Gnochetti sardi* are a larger, longer version of malloreddus, made by cutting the dough into 2 cm lengths before shaping.

You can buy good dried malloreddus, but if you'd like to make your own, try to find a gnocchi board, a special corrugated board to roll the pasta along; they're available from some speciality food stores. In some areas malloreddus were rolled on a device called a *ciurili*, which looks a bit like a drum sieve but instead of the wire mesh has rows of very closely spaced, thin canes that the dough is rolled along to get the traditional rough surface and folded shape.

CICIONES PASTA WITH PORK SAUSAGE SAUCE

CICIONES ALLA CAMPIDANESE

Cicio means 'fat', and these fat little pasta shapes are halfway between gnocchi and malloreddus. Saffron is used in a lot of Sardinian dishes, but more commonly in the south than the north, where I come from. Here I make an exception and use it to give the pasta dough a lovely golden colour. *Campidanese* means 'from the Campidano area', the plains of southern Sardinia where a lot of vegetables are grown, especially tomatoes; this sauce is typical of that region.

SERVES 4 AS A FIRST COURSE

½ quantity Fresh Pasta Dough #3 with saffron (see page 217), not rolled through pasta machine
tipo 00 flour, for dusting
¼ cup (60 ml) extra virgin olive oil, plus extra for drizzling
1 small brown onion, finely diced
1 small carrot, peeled and finely diced
1 stalk celery heart, finely diced
250 g Italian-style pork sausages, skins removed
1 tablespoon tomato paste (purée)
¼ teaspoon saffron threads
2 bay leaves
1 sprig rosemary
400 g canned peeled tomatoes, drained and squashed
5 basil leaves, torn
salt flakes, to taste
fine sea salt, for pasta water
80 g aged Pecorino Sardo, freshly grated

Place pasta dough on a clean, dry workbench and, using the palms of your hands, roll it into logs, about 1 cm wide; only if dough starts to stick to the bench, dust bench very lightly with a little flour. If it starts to slip on the bench rather than roll, put a drop of water on your hands. Cut pasta logs into small pieces about the size of a chickpea. Sprinkle with flour and set aside.

Heat a large frying pan over medium heat, add oil and, when hot, add onion, carrot and celery and cook until soft and slightly coloured. Add sausage meat, spread it out evenly in the pan and cook, without stirring, for 5 minutes. Then, using a wooden spoon to break it up, turn the meat over and cook the other side for a few minutes, until browned all over. Stir in tomato paste, saffron, bay leaves and rosemary and cook for a further minute. Add tomatoes, basil and 1 cup (250 ml) water and bring to the boil. Reduce heat and simmer for about 45 minutes, stirring occasionally and crushing the meat slightly, until sauce is quite thick; if it dries out too much, add a little more water. Taste and season lightly with salt flakes, if needed.

Bring a large saucepan of water to the boil, add fine sea salt, then pasta and boil for about 10–12 minutes from the time the water returns to the boil, until tender. Drain well, reserving some of the cooking water. Toss the pecorino through the pasta, a little at a time, then add the sauce and toss for a minute or two to coat well. If it seems a bit dry, add a couple of tablespoons of reserved cooking water and stir it through well, adding a little more if necessary to give a glossy appearance. Drizzle with olive oil and serve immediately.

Saffron

Saffron was likely introduced to Sardinia by the Phoenicians around 700BC and has long been used to colour, scent and flavour pastas, ragùs and desserts. Sardinian saffron, grown in the province of Medio Campidano around San Gavino Monreale, is highly regarded and was granted PDO (Protected Designation of Origin) status by the European Union in 2009. If you can't buy Sardinian saffron, make sure you buy authentic saffron threads – not powder, which can too easily be adulterated. Good saffron is expensive, but just a pinch gives great results.

POTATO AND MINT RAVIOLI WITH BURNT BUTTER AND SAGE

CULURZONES

SERVES 8 AS A FIRST COURSE

700 g desiree potatoes
fine sea salt, for potato and pasta water
2 eggs, well beaten
60 g aged Pecorino Sardo, freshly grated,
    plus extra for serving
handful finely sliced mint leaves
pinch freshly grated nutmeg
salt flakes, to taste
½ quantity Fresh Pasta Dough #2
    (see page 217), passed through
    pasta machine four times
tipo oo flour, for dusting
200 g butter
3 tablespoons sage leaves
juice of ½ lemon, strained
2 tablespoons finely sliced
    flat-leaf parsley leaves

Note

Use the off-cuts from cutting the pasta
rounds to make stracci (see page 150).

I remember my Zia (Aunt) Maria serving culurzones on a big platter: she'd layer some pasta, then sauce, then more pasta, and more sauce and so on, so that when people served themselves everyone had some sauce, not just the people taking the top layer. We tend to call all filled pasta culurzones in my dialect, but these are true culurzones, filled with potato and mint and shaped like an ear of wheat; they're traditionally served with Passata (see page 218) and pecorino, but this is how I serve them at the restaurant. It takes a lot of practice to perfect the technique for shaping these pastas, so don't despair, just keep practising and remember, they'll taste great, even if they don't look perfect.

Cook potatoes, in their skins, in boiling salted water for about 30 minutes, until a wooden skewer can be inserted without any resistance. Drain and pass through a potato ricer. Mix egg, pecorino, mint, nutmeg and salt flakes through the potato. Set aside to cool, then put into a piping bag.

Meanwhile, lay pasta sheet on a clean, lightly floured workbench and cut out 7 cm rounds. Dust lightly with flour, then place on a lightly floured tray and cover with plastic wrap.

Place a pasta round on the fingers of one hand and pipe a thick sausage of the potato filling along its centre. Turn the bottom of the dough over the end of the filling then, using the thumb of the other hand, pinch a small fold of dough over from one side, then, without moving your thumb, use the first finger to pinch a small fold of dough over from the other side. Continue making tiny pinches from alternate sides without moving either the thumb or other finger when you aren't using them, sealing across the top of the parcel to create a pleated effect and squeezing any excess filling out of the end. Twist the end to seal it off. Carry on shaping the culurzones, trying not to press down (or too much filling will be pushed out) and keeping the pinches as small as possible, until all the pasta rounds and filling have been used.

Bring a large saucepan of water to the boil, add fine sea salt, then half the culurzones and cook at a gentle boil for 3–5 minutes from the time the water returns to the boil, until tender. Using a slotted spoon, scoop them out and place in a colander to drain well. Repeat with remaining culurzones.

Meanwhile, put butter and sage in a large frying pan over low heat until butter melts, then continue cooking until butter is golden. Add lemon juice and parsley and remove from heat.

Add culurzones to the hot butter mixture, stirring to coat them thoroughly, then serve on a plate with extra grated pecorino scattered over the top.

LEMON TAGLIERINI WITH SEA URCHIN AND ARTICHOKE CREAM

TAGLIERINI AL LIMONE CON POLPA DI RICCI E CREMA DI CARCIOFI

½ quantity Fresh Pasta Dough #1
    (see page 217) with lemon zest, passed
    through pasta machine six times
tipo 00 flour, for dusting
fine sea salt, for pasta water
½ cup (125 ml) extra virgin olive oil,
    plus extra for drizzling
90 g sea urchin roe, roughly chopped

ARTICHOKE CREAM

2 lemons, halved
6 globe artichokes
5 bay leaves
10 black peppercorns
1 stalk celery heart, roughly chopped
3 tablespoons flat-leaf parsley leaves
salt flakes and freshly ground white
    pepper, to taste
½ cup (125 ml) extra virgin olive oil

Once when we were on holiday in Sardinia, my sister, Alessandra, took us to a very remote restaurant near Cuglieri, in central Sardinia. To start with, they brought us a big basket of bread and a bowl full of ice. Nestled into the ice were live sea urchins, freshly cracked, with extra virgin olive oil drizzled over the roe. We ate the bread dipped into the roe and oil, and I've never forgotten the pure intensity of the flavour. Sea urchin roe is available from some fishmongers. Sea urchin roe should never be heated – just place it on top of the pasta and ask diners to mix it through for themselves at the table You'll need a taglierini attachment for your pasta machine to make this very thin pasta, which is like flattened angel hair. If you don't have the correct attachment, use the thinnest attachment you have. In Sardinia the dough is folded up into a flattened roll and cut into very fine strips with a knife, but that takes a very sharp knife and a lot of practice.

First make the artichoke cream. Add lemon juice and the squeezed lemon halves to a large saucepan of cold water. Working with one artichoke at a time, peel off the dark outer leaves until you reach the tender light-green ones. Using a sharp paring knife, cut off the top third of the artichoke. Trim the stalk so that it's just a couple of centimetres long, then peel it. Cut artichoke in half and, using a teaspoon, scoop any hairy choke out of the centre. Rub artichoke with one of the lemon halves from the pan, then place in the acidulated water. Repeat with remaining artichokes. Add bay leaves, peppercorns and celery and cover with a round of baking paper. Bring to the boil, then reduce heat and simmer for about 25–35 minutes, until a wooden skewer can be inserted into the base of the artichokes without any resistance. Drain artichokes and place in a food processor with parsley, salt and pepper and pulse until well chopped. With the machine running, drizzle in oil and process until smooth. Pass through a fine sieve.

Cut pasta sheets into 24 cm lengths and trim the sides. Pass sheets through a taglierini attachment on the pasta machine. Toss with a little flour and set aside.

Bring a large saucepan of water to the boil and add salt. Shake taglierini gently to separate the strands then add to the water and boil for 1–2 minutes from the time the water returns to the boil, until tender.

Meanwhile, heat a large frying pan, add oil and, when hot, use tongs or a spaghetti spoon to lift the cooked pasta from the boiling water into the frying pan. Add about ⅓ cup (80 ml) of the pasta cooking water and toss thoroughly to give a creamy consistency, adding a little more water if it seems too dry.

Divide artichoke cream among six plates. Arrange taglierini along the middle, top with sea urchin roe, drizzle with olive oil and mix well before eating.

TROFIE PASTA CARLOFORTE-STYLE

TROFIE ALLA CARLOFORTINA

SERVES 6 AS A FIRST COURSE

½ quantity Fresh Pasta Dough #1
   (see page 217), passed through
   pasta machine five times
tipo 00 flour, for dusting
50 ml extra virgin olive oil
½ brown onion, finely chopped
200 g yellow grape tomatoes,
   tops cut off, halved
salt flakes, to taste
fine sea salt, for pasta water
300 g sashimi-grade tuna,
   cut into 2 cm cubes

BASIL CREAM

20 basil leaves
100 ml extra virgin olive oil
50 g pine nuts
2 cloves garlic, peeled
salt flakes, to taste

Trofie is a pasta from Liguria. I've used it in this dish because of the strong Genovese influence in Carloforte, a town on San Pietro island, just off the southwestern coast of mainland Sardinia. Carloforte was founded in the 18th century by coral fishermen from Pegli, near Genoa in Liguria, and their descendants still speak a Ligurian dialect. The golden grape tomatoes give this dish a lovely colour; you could also use red tomatoes of course, but if using larger tomatoes, peel and deseed them first. If you don't want to make your own pasta, you can use 500 g dried trofie or a similar pasta, such as strozzapreti, cavatelli or casarecce.

Lay pasta sheets on a clean, lightly floured workbench and cut into strips about 4 cm long and 5 mm wide. Roll each strip between the palms of your hands to form a thin spiral. Place trofie on a tray and sprinkle lightly with flour.

To make the basil cream, put all ingredients in a food processor and process until well combined and creamy. Set aside.

Heat a frying pan over low heat, add oil and, when hot, cook onion until soft but not coloured. Add tomatoes and cook over medium heat for about 10 minutes, occasionally stirring and crushing the tomatoes with a wooden spoon, until sauce thickens slightly. Stir in salt flakes then place in a blender and purée until smooth. Pass through a fine sieve into a large clean saucepan.

Meanwhile, bring a large saucepan of water to the boil, add fine sea salt, then trofie and boil for about 6 minutes from the time the water returns to the boil, until tender. Drain well, reserving some of the cooking water.

Place tomato sauce over low heat. Add pasta and toss for a minute or two to coat, then add a couple of tablespoons of the reserved cooking water and stir well, adding a little more if necessary to give a glossy appearance.

Remove from heat, add the tuna and toss through the pasta for about 1 minute, just until the outside of the tuna turns opaque.

Serve the trofie in pasta bowls, drizzled with a spoonful of basil cream.

FUSILLI WITH SQUID AND SAFFRON SAUCE

FUSILLI CON RAGÙ DI CALAMARI E ZAFFERANO

SERVES 6 AS A FIRST COURSE

6 squid, cleaned and skinned
⅓ cup (80 ml) extra virgin olive oil,
   plus extra for drizzling
2 golden shallots, finely diced
1 stalk celery heart, finely diced
1 tablespoon salted baby capers,
   rinsed and dried
2 tablespoons Vermentino (see page 219)
   or other dry white wine
125 g canned peeled tomatoes,
   drained and lightly squashed
1 teaspoon tomato paste (purée)
¼ teaspoon saffron threads
½ teaspoon dried Greek oregano
   (see page 220)
fine sea salt, for pasta water
500 g fusilli
20 Ligurian olives, pitted
salt flakes and freshly ground black
   pepper, to taste
1 tablespoon finely sliced basil leaves

It's easy enough to make fresh pasta, but every Sardinian household has packets of dried pasta in the cupboard as a stand-by for quick meals. When I was a kid, we went to school six days a week, but finished just after 1 p.m., then we'd all race home for a late lunch. Pasta is my brother Cristiano's favourite food, and Mum would often have a dish of dried pasta with a simple sauce on the table waiting for us after school.

Seafood ragùs like this are popular all over the Italian coast. This one, which I cook at the restaurant, has a Sardinian flavour because of the Vermentino wine and saffron. I use dried Greek oregano rather than fresh here, because it is more like the wild oregano that grows all over Sardinia. Instead of fusilli, you could use any other short pasta, such as trofie; hand-rolled macaroni (see page 32) is also fabulous with this sauce.

Cut squid hood open. Using the back of a knife, scrape off the membrane from inside the hood. Trim off the base and slice the hood into thin strips; halve tentacles.

Heat a large frying pan over medium heat, add oil and, when hot, cook shallots and celery until soft but not coloured. Add capers and cook for a further 2 minutes, then add wine and cook for a minute or two until it starts to boil. Add squid and cook for 10 minutes. Add tomatoes, tomato paste, saffron and oregano. Bring to the boil, then reduce heat and cook for a further 30 minutes or so, until squid is tender.

Meanwhile, bring a large saucepan of water to the boil, add fine sea salt, then fusilli and boil for about 8–10 minutes from the time the water returns to the boil, until al dente.

When pasta is almost ready, stir olives, salt flakes and pepper through the sauce, then stir in the basil.

Drain pasta well, reserving some of the cooking water. Add pasta to the sauce and toss for a minute or two to coat, then add a couple of tablespoons of the reserved cooking water and stir it through well, adding a little more if necessary to give a creamy consistency. Drizzle with olive oil and serve immediately.

HAND-ROLLED MACARONI with CRAB AND GRAPE TOMATOES

MACCARRONES DE BUSA CON POLPA DI GRANCHIO E POMODORINI

SERVES 4 AS A FIRST COURSE

¼ cup (60 ml) extra virgin olive oil,
    plus extra for drizzling
1 clove garlic, finely sliced
1 small red chilli, finely sliced
24 grape tomatoes, tops cut off,
    halved
salt flakes, to taste
250 g raw crabmeat
2 tablespoons Cinzano bianco
fine sea salt, for pasta water
1 tablespoon finely sliced
    flat-leaf parsley leaves

MACARONI DOUGH

250 g semolina flour (see page 220),
    plus extra for kneading and dusting
pinch fine sea salt
about 100 ml warm water

The Sardinian word *busa* comes from *bus*, the Arabic name for a type of reed which grows in the Mediterranean and around which this pasta was originally rolled; it's now the name given to the stick or narrow metal rod used to shape the pasta. In my dialect we call this pasta *maccarrones a ferrittu – ferrittu* means knitting needle, which is what we use to roll this pasta. However, it's easier to roll on a square rod rather than a round one, which tends to slide rather than roll. A thin metal rod about 2–3 mm in diameter is ideal: either snip the end off a metal skewer with a square profile, or look for an appropriately sized rod in the steel section of a hardware store. It's a tricky business picking meat from raw crabs, but raw crabmeat is available from some fishmongers. If only cooked crabmeat is available, squeeze it well to remove any excess moisture and add it to the sauce at the end of the cooking.

First make the macaroni dough. Sift the flour and salt into the bowl of an electric mixer fitted with a dough hook. With the machine running, gradually pour in just enough warm water to form a firm dough – it may not completely come together (you need a very dry dough, otherwise it will stick and be impossible to slide off the *busa*). Tip the dough onto a clean, lightly floured workbench and knead with the heels of your hands; if it feels too dry to come together, wet your hands and continue kneading. Keep wetting your hands and kneading until the dough just comes together – it doesn't take much extra water for the dough to become too soft. Knead the dough for 5–10 minutes until smooth, then roll into a ball, wrap in plastic wrap and set aside for about 1 hour.

Pull off a piece of dough about the size of a large hazelnut and wrap it around the centre of the rod (*busa*). Using the palm of one hand, roll it back and forth on a clean, dry workbench; it's important that you do not flour the workbench, or the dough will slide instead of rolling. As the macaroni gets longer, use both palms to roll it into a long, hollow strip. Gently ease it off the rod and place on a clean, flour-dusted tray. Repeat with remaining dough.

Heat a large frying pan over low heat, add oil and, when hot, cook garlic and chilli for about 1 minute, until soft but not coloured. Add tomatoes and cook for a further 3 minutes, crushing gently with a wooden spoon. Add salt flakes and crabmeat and cook, stirring gently until the meat turns white, about 1 minute. Add Cinzano bianco and cook for 1 minute. Remove pan from heat and set aside.

Bring a large saucepan of water to the boil, add fine sea salt, then the macaroni and boil for about 6 minutes from the time the water returns to the boil, until tender. Drain well, reserving some of the cooking water.

Add pasta to the frying pan and return to low heat. Add parsley and toss for a minute or two to coat the macaroni well, then add a couple of tablespoons of the reserved cooking water and stir it through well, adding a little more if necessary to give a creamy consistency.

Drizzle with olive oil and serve immediately.

LOMBRICHI PASTA WITH OCTOPUS SAUCE

LOMBRICHI CON SUGO DI POLPI

SERVES 4 AS A FIRST COURSE

1 quantity Fresh Pasta Dough #3
   (see page 217) with cuttlefish ink,
   not rolled through pasta machine
tipo 00 flour, for dusting
fine sea salt, for pasta water
extra virgin olive oil, for drizzling

OCTOPUS SAUCE

900 g octopus, cleaned
⅓ cup (80 ml) extra virgin olive oil
1 clove garlic, finely sliced
1 small red chilli, finely sliced
2 tablespoons tomato paste (purée)
¼ teaspoon saffron threads
1 tablespoon finely sliced
   flat-leaf parsley leaves
1 tablespoon finely sliced basil leaves
½ tablespoon oregano leaves
about 2 cups (500 ml) Fish Stock
   (see page 213)
salt flakes, to taste

Lombrichi **is the Italian word for 'worms' (the name of another pasta, vermicelli, means 'small worms'), and this dough is made with cuttlefish ink so the worms are the right colour. If you don't want to cook the pasta straight away it can be dried, but because it's a dense pasta, the dried version will take about 15 minutes to cook.**

First make the octopus sauce. Slice each tentacle into rounds, split head open and cut into fine strips. Heat a saucepan over medium heat, add oil and, when hot, add garlic and chilli and cook for 1 minute, until garlic begins to soften. Stir in octopus, increase heat to medium–high and cook for 10–12 minutes, until the liquid it gives off has mostly evaporated. Stir in tomato paste, saffron, parsley, basil, oregano, half the stock and salt flakes. Bring to the boil, then reduce heat and simmer for about 45 minutes, until octopus is tender and sauce is reduced to the thickness of pouring cream, stirring occasionally and adding extra stock, a little at a time, as the sauce starts to stick and dry out – you may not need all the stock.

Meanwhile, unwrap the pasta dough and pinch off a walnut-sized piece. Place on a clean, dry workbench and, using the palms of your hands, roll it into a long 'worm' about 3 mm thick. If the dough starts to stick to the bench, dust bench very lightly with a little flour; if it starts to slip on the bench rather than roll, put a drop of water on your hands. Cut into 5 cm lengths, dust lightly with flour and place on a tray. Repeat with remaining dough.

Bring a large saucepan of water to the boil, add salt, then pasta and boil for 7–8 minutes from the time the water returns to the boil, until tender. Drain well, reserving some of the cooking water. Return pasta to the saucepan, add most of the sauce and a drizzle of olive oil and toss for a minute or two to coat well. If it seems a little dry, add a couple of tablespoons of the reserved cooking water and stir it through well, adding a little more if necessary to give a glossy appearance.

Divide among pasta bowls and drizzle with a little olive oil. Serve remaining sauce in a bowl for those who like their pasta extra saucy.

TALLUZZAS PASTA WITH BRAISED BABY GOAT

TALLUZZAS CON SUGO DI CAPRETTO

SERVES 12 AS A FIRST COURSE

1 × 2 kg shoulder baby goat,
    cut into 8 pieces
1 quantity Fresh Pasta Dough #1
    (see page 217), passed through
    pasta machine four times
tipo 00 flour, for dusting
½ cup (125 ml) extra virgin olive oil,
    plus extra for drizzling
1 small brown onion, diced
1 carrot, peeled and diced
1 stalk celery heart, diced
2 cloves garlic, sliced
1 litre Chicken Stock (see page 214)
salt flakes and freshly ground black
    pepper, to taste
fine sea salt, for pasta water
50 g butter, diced
finely grated zest of 1 lemon
100 g young Pecorino Sardo,
    freshly grated

RED WINE MARINADE

1 litre Cannonau (see page 219)
    or other full-bodied red wine
2 sprigs rosemary, torn
2 bay leaves
2 sprigs thyme, torn
10 black peppercorns

Since it's difficult to buy less than one shoulder of goat, this dish serves a lot of people – it's a great dish to make for a get-together with family or friends. Any leftover sauce will keep refrigerated for a few days and tastes even better reheated. You'll need to start this recipe a day ahead, to give the meat time to marinate. This is a rustic dish so the pasta dough doesn't need to be rolled very finely – it has a lovely, almost chewy, texture. Most halal butchers stock goat, and some other butchers will order it in on request, but you could use lamb if goat is unavailable.

Combine all the red wine marinade ingredients. Add goat to marinade, cover and refrigerate for 24 hours, turning 3 or 4 times so that all meat spends time in contact with the marinade.

Remove goat from the fridge 1–2 hours before cooking and set aside in a cool place to come to room temperature.

Place pasta sheets on a clean, lightly floured workbench and cut into 5 cm rounds. Set aside.

Remove goat from marinade and pat dry. Dust meat well in flour, shaking off any excess. Heat half the oil in a large frying pan over medium heat, add half the goat and cook for about 4 minutes, turning as needed to brown all sides. Transfer meat to a roasting tin, skin-side down. Fry remaining goat, adding a little more oil if necessary. Wipe out frying pan with paper towel.

Preheat oven to 180°C.

Add remaining oil to the frying pan. When hot, add onion, carrot, celery and garlic and cook over medium heat, stirring occasionally, for 5–7 minutes, until soft and starting to colour. Add marinade, bring to the boil, then reduce heat and simmer for 5 minutes. Add stock and return to the boil.

Sprinkle goat with salt flakes and carefully pour vegetables and liquid over it. Cover tightly with a double layer of foil (see page 222) and cook in oven for about 2 hours, until meat is so tender that you can break it apart with a spoon. Remove from oven, take the meat out of the tin and, when cool enough to handle, strip the flesh from the bones in large chunks and set aside. Discard bones.

Place roasting tin on the stovetop over high heat and bring to the boil. Skim off any fat that rises to the surface, remove bay leaves and rosemary and thyme stalks and boil until the sauce is reduced to the thickness of pouring cream. Add salt flakes and pepper. Remove from heat, return meat to the sauce and stir to combine well. Cover and keep warm.

Bring a large saucepan of water to the boil, add fine sea salt, then pasta and boil for about 3 minutes from the time the water returns to the boil, until tender. Drain well, reserving some of the cooking water. Return the pasta to the saucepan, add most of the sauce and toss for a minute or two to coat well. Add the butter, half the lemon zest and a drizzle of olive oil and toss well to combine. If it seems a bit dry add a couple of tablespoons of the reserved cooking water and stir it through well, adding a little more cooking water if necessary; take care not to make the sauce watery.

Divide among pasta bowls. Sprinkle with pecorino and the rest of the lemon zest. Serve with the remaining sauce in a separate bowl for those who like their pasta extra saucy.

FREGOLA COOKED RISOTTO-STYLE WITH SEAFOOD SAUCE

FREGOLA RISOTATTA CON RAGÙ DI PESCE

SERVES 6 AS A FIRST COURSE

120 g squid, cleaned and skinned

24 blue mussels, scrubbed lightly
with a scourer

about 1.7 litres Fish Stock (see page 213)

½ cup (125 ml) extra virgin olive oil,
plus extra for drizzling

1 small brown onion, finely diced

1 clove garlic, finely sliced

60 g baby octopus, cleaned and
finely diced

120 g raw prawns, peeled, deveined and
finely diced

8 saucer scallops, trimmed and finely diced

30 ml Vermentino (see page 219)
or other dry white wine

40 g tomato paste (purée)

3 tablespoons finely sliced
flat-leaf parsley leaves

1 tablespoon finely sliced basil leaves

1 tablespoon oregano leaves

½ tablespoon thyme leaves

100 g butter

400 g fregola (see page 106)

salt flakes and freshly ground black
pepper, to taste

Rather than being boiled, pasta – especially small shapes like fregola – can be cooked in the same way as risotto, with the liquid being stirred into it a little at a time until the pasta is tender. This makes for a particularly tasty dish as the pasta absorbs all of the flavour of the stock or sauce in which it's cooked.

Cut squid hood open. Using the back of a knife, scrape off the membrane from inside the hood. Trim off the base and dice the hood finely; halve tentacles.

Place mussels in a large frying pan over high heat. Cover, shake pan well and cook for about 3 minutes, shaking occasionally, until most of the shells open. Remove from heat. Fish out any mussels that haven't opened and, using a blunt knife such as a butter knife, gently prise them open: if the meat is plump and intact on one side of the shell, use them; otherwise discard them. Remove meat from shells and pull off the 'beards'. Finely dice mussel meat. Strain cooking juices into a saucepan, add stock and heat until simmering, then remove from heat and cover to keep warm.

Heat a large frying pan, add half the oil and, when hot, add onion and garlic and cook over medium heat until soft and slightly coloured. Add squid and octopus and cook for about 5 minutes, until they colour. Add prawns and scallops and cook for a further 2 minutes. Add wine and cook for a minute or two until it starts to boil. Add tomato paste, parsley, basil, oregano, thyme and just enough stock to cover the seafood (about 200 ml). Bring to a simmer and cook over low heat for about 15 minutes, until most of the stock has evaporated. Stir through chopped mussel meat, then remove from heat and set aside.

Pour remaining stock into a small saucepan and bring to the boil, then reduce heat to its lowest setting and keep warm.

Heat a large saucepan over medium heat, add remaining oil and 30 g of the butter. When butter melts, add fregola and toss to coat well. Add a couple of ladlefuls of the hot stock, stirring continuously. When the stock is almost completely absorbed, stir in a couple more ladlefuls and continue in this way until the fregola is al dente, about 12 minutes altogether – you may not need all the stock.

Remove from heat, add seafood mixture and stir to combine well. Add salt and pepper, the remaining butter and a drizzle of olive oil and stir vigorously – you may need to add a little more hot stock to ensure it has a soft, slightly soupy consistency.

Divide among six shallow bowls, tapping the base of each one to spread the fregola out. Drizzle with olive oil and serve.

RICE WITH PORK AND WHITE WINE

RISO ALLA SARDA CON VERNACCIA

SERVES 4 AS A FIRST COURSE

250 g pork loin, cut into 1 cm dice
salt flakes and freshly ground black
   pepper, to taste
¼ cup (60 ml) red wine vinegar
2 cloves garlic, finely sliced
1.5 litres Veal Stock (see page 214)
¼ cup (60 ml) extra virgin olive oil
1 small brown onion, finely diced
280 g carnaroli rice
½ cup (125 ml) Vernaccia di Oristano
   (see page 219) or other dry white wine
100 g aged Pecorino Sardo, freshly grated
1 tablespoon finely sliced sage,
   plus a few whole leaves

There are many traditional rice dishes in Italy other than risotto. Rice has been grown in Sardinia for many centuries and this is how we traditionally cook it; it's not risotto, because it isn't finished with butter (*mantecare* in Italian). The name for this dish in my dialect is *Risu cun Pulpedda* (other dialects would say *purpuzza*); *pulpedda* are the little bits of pork meat leftover from making the sausages after the pig has been killed (see page 131). I remember eating this as a kid and my mother telling us to flatten it with our fork and start from the outside of the plate, which is colder, and eat towards the centre, which is hotter, or we'd burn our mouths. You'll need to start this recipe a day ahead to give the pork time to marinate.

Place pork in a glass or ceramic bowl, sprinkle with salt and pepper, then add vinegar and garlic. Mix well, then cover and refrigerate overnight.

Pour stock into a small saucepan, bring to the boil, then reduce heat to its lowest setting and keep warm.

Heat a saucepan over medium heat, add oil and, when hot, cook onion for about 5 minutes, until soft and slightly golden. Drain pork well and add to the onion. Increase heat to high and cook for 3–5 minutes, until the meat is well browned on all sides.

Reduce heat to medium, add rice and stir for about a minute, until the rice is hot and completely coated in oil. Increase heat to high, add wine and stir for a minute or two until it starts to boil. Reduce heat to low–medium and add a couple of ladlefuls of the hot stock, stirring continuously. When the stock is almost completely absorbed, stir in a couple more ladlefuls and continue in this way until the rice is tender, about 20 minutes altogether – you may not need all the stock.

Remove from the heat and stir in pecorino and sliced sage, plus salt and pepper. Divide among four bowls, garnish with whole sage leaves and serve.

DURE

Vegetables

As a *cucina rustica* ('rustic cuisine'), Sardinian cooking features a lot of vegetable dishes. In peasant cultures, animals were kept to provide milk, wool and eggs, or to help pull ploughs, and so were only killed for meat at the end of their working life or for special occasions. Meat was a luxury food and vegetables and grains were typically added to dishes to help make a little go a long way. Predominantly vegetable dishes are often flavoured with just a little meat in the form of cured pork, such as guanciale, or seasoned with Sardinia's famous bottarga (dried mullet roe; see page 93). Meat stocks, leftover from boiling a chicken or a piece of mutton, are also used to add depth of flavour to simple vegetable dishes.

Most of Sardinia's fruit and vegetables are grown on the fertile plains of Campidano in the south, as well as in the backyard plots most families still cultivate throughout the island. We eat whatever vegetables are in season, making a feast of them and enjoying them in many different ways, knowing it'll be another year until that season comes around again. Artichokes are particularly popular; being a thistle, they seem naturally acclimatised to Sardinia's dry, rocky ground. They're native to the Mediterranean, having evolved from wild cardoons, which are also still popular in Sardinia. The Arabs in North Africa grew them extensively, leading to the Arabic name, *al-qarchuf*, being adopted into Italian as *carciofi* and into English as artichoke. They're at their best in late autumn and winter and during this time many different dishes using them appear on restaurant menus and in home kitchens.

Zucchini are also popular; once planted they grow almost wild, producing abundant vegetables and beautiful bright yellow flowers. In the spirit of wasting nothing, these flowers are also used, shredded into dishes or left whole and stuffed with various fillings then deep-fried. Eggplants are popular in summer, along with deep red, flavourful tomatoes.

Celery and fennel are used all over Italy for their fleshy stalks and greenery. In Sardinia we use them in salads as well as cooked dishes, and often collect wild fennel from the hillsides. Celery is popular in home vegetable patches; I prefer to use the tender inner stalks (heart) for eating, keeping the coarser outer stalks for stocks and marinades.

We grow all sorts of beans, including borlotti and broad beans, which are delicious when they're young and tender. Later in the season, when they get larger and tougher, they're often dried for use once their season is over. Root vegetables aren't common in Sardinia, with the exception of radishes, which we often add to salads – and, of course, potatoes.

Mint is Sardinia's most ubiquitous herb, growing like a weed, followed closely by rosemary, hedges of which are used to divide fields. Sage, thyme, parsley, basil, marjoram and oregano also add flavour to many dishes, as do myrtle leaves (see page 143), which are used in much the same way many other cuisines use bay leaves – added to almost every pot.

Most of the dishes in this chapter can be served as part of an antipasto, and many make good accompaniments to other dishes.

See also
- Potato and Mint Ravioli with Burnt Buttter and Sage (page 24) in 'Pasta and Rice'
- Artichoke Cream (Lemon Taglierini with Sea Urchin and Artichoke Cream; page 26) in 'Pasta and Rice'
- Eggplant Purée (Crumbed Sardines with Pecorino and Eggplant Purée; page 75) in 'Seafood'
- Slow-cooked Red Capsicum (Scorpionfish Fillets with Slow-cooked Red Capsicum and Mussels; page 78) in 'Seafood'
- Braised Fennel (Rack of Lamb with Braised Fennel and Green Sauce; page 115) in 'Meat and Poultry'
- Fregola and Olive Salad (Lamb Rump with Fregola and Olive Salad; page 116) in 'Meat and Poultry'
- Chestnut Purée (Roast Duck with Chestnuts; page 148) in 'Hunting and Foraging'

FRIED ARTICHOKES

CARCIOFI FRITTI

SERVES 4 AS A FIRST COURSE

2 lemons, halved
8 globe artichokes
  or 16 baby globe artichokes
vegetable oil, for deep-frying
200 g coarse semolina (see page 221)
salt flakes, to taste

Globe artichokes are a thistle native to the Mediterranean, and the part we eat is the immature flower head or bud. They should be very firm when you buy them – and if they are young enough, there won't be any hairy choke in the centre to deal with. Artichokes do take a bit of work to prepare, but I think they're well worth it. They oxidise easily and so need to be put into acidulated water as soon as they're cut, to prevent them discolouring.

Add lemon juice and squeezed lemon halves to a large bowl of cold water. Working with one artichoke at a time, peel off the dark outer leaves until you reach the tender light-green ones. Using a sharp paring knife, cut off the top third of the artichoke. Trim the stalk so that it's just a couple of centimetres long, then peel it. Using a teaspoon, scoop any hairy choke out of the centre of the artichoke. Rub the artichoke with one of the lemon halves from the bowl of water, then place in the acidulated water. Repeat with remaining artichokes.

Heat vegetable oil to 160°C (if you don't have a deep-frying thermometer, test the temperature of the oil by dipping the handle of a wooden spoon into it – when bubbles form around the spoon, the oil is hot enough).

Meanwhile, cut artichokes in half if large, dry well and toss in semolina to coat. Carefully lower into hot oil and deep-fry for 2–3 minutes, until underside is golden, then turn and fry other side for another 2–3 minutes. Drain on paper towel, sprinkle with salt and serve.

ZUCCHINI FRITTERS WITH MINT AND PECORINO

FRITELLE DI ZUCCHINE CON MENTA E PECORINO

SERVES 4 AS A FIRST COURSE

¼ cup (35 g) plain flour
¼ cup (60 ml) sparkling water
3 eggs, lightly beaten
60 g aged Pecorino Sardo, freshly grated
1 tablespoon finely sliced mint leaves
1 tablespoon marjoram leaves
salt flakes and freshly ground black
  pepper, to taste
4 zucchini (courgettes), ends trimmed,
  cut into matchsticks
vegetable oil, for deep-frying

At left: Zucchini Fritters with Mint and Pecorino (this page); on plate: Fried Artichokes (this page) and Deep-fried Stuffed Zucchini Flowers (page 48)

Most Sardinians grow at least a few fruit and vegetables at home, and zucchini plants produce an abundant crop. Since mint grows like a weed in most gardens and there's always pecorino in the pantry, this makes a simple inexpensive snack or start to a meal using what's on hand. And deep-frying, which is popular in Sardinian cooking, results in a great texture and makes everything taste better. Artichokes are also great done this way. For an elegant presentation, serve these fritters on a bed of mint and marjoram leaves.

Sift flour into a bowl. Slowly pour in the sparkling water, whisking all the time, to form a smooth batter. Slowly pour in the egg, still whisking constantly, until completely incorporated. Stir in pecorino, mint, marjoram, salt and pepper. Gently fold in the zucchini, being carefully not to break it up.

Heat vegetable oil to 160°C (if you don't have a deep-frying thermometer, test the temperature of the oil by dipping the handle of a wooden spoon into it – when bubbles form around the spoon, the oil is hot enough).

Scoop up a tablespoonful of zucchini mixture and, using a second tablespoon, carefully slide it into hot oil and deep-fry for about 4 minutes, until underside is golden, then turn and fry other side for 2–3 minutes, until golden. Drain on paper towel. Sprinkle with salt and serve warm or at room temperature.

DEEP-FRIED STUFFED ZUCCHINI FLOWERS

FIORI DI ZUCCHINE RIPIENI E FRITTI

SERVES 6 AS A FIRST COURSE

30 g shelled walnuts, toasted
    (see page 222) and finely chopped
3 tablespoons finely sliced
    flat-leaf parsley leaves
2 tablespoons finely sliced mint leaves
3 tablespoons finely sliced basil leaves
finely grated zest of ½ lemon
generous pinch dried chilli flakes
salt flakes, to taste
175 g fresh goat's cheese
18 female zucchini (courgette) flowers,
    with baby zucchini attached
vegetable oil, for deep-frying
3 lemons, cut into cheeks

BATTER

250 g self-raising flour
500 ml chilled water

I know stuffed zucchini flowers appear everywhere these days, but I do think these ones (in the photo on page 46) are special, with their stuffing of goat's cheese, walnuts, lemon zest, mint and a touch of dried chilli. If you grow zucchini in the garden, pick the flowers in the morning when they're already open; they close soon after being cut, so the trick is to cut them, remove the stamen and stuff them quickly, then they close around the stuffing.

To make the batter, sift flour into a bowl and slowly pour in the water, whisking constantly to form a smooth batter. Pass through a fine sieve and set aside to rest.

Preheat oven to 100°C.

To make the stuffing for the zucchini flowers, mash the walnuts, parsley, mint, basil, lemon zest, chilli flakes and salt into the goat's cheese with a fork until well combined.

Trim the base off the small zucchini attached to the flowers. Gently open the flower petals, being careful not to bruise them, and pinch off the stamen from the centre of each flower. Place a teaspoon of stuffing inside each flower and gently fold the petals back around it.

Heat vegetable oil to 160°C (if you don't have a deep-frying thermometer, test the temperature of the oil by dipping the handle of a wooden spoon into it – when bubbles form around the spoon, the oil is hot enough).

Whisk batter again. Holding a flower by its zucchini, dip it into the batter and gently wipe up the side of the bowl to remove excess batter. Lower carefully into hot oil. Repeat with remaining flowers, deep-frying them in batches for about 2 minutes, until underside is golden, then turning and frying the other side for a minute or two, until golden. Drain on paper towel.

Serve sprinkled with salt, with a lemon cheek on the side.

STUFFED ZUCCHINI

ZUCCHINE RIPIENE

SERVES 4 AS A FIRST COURSE

4 zucchini (courgettes)
extra virgin olive oil, for shallow-frying
1 clove garlic, finely sliced
2 anchovy fillets in oil, drained,
   finely chopped
5 grape tomatoes, tops cut off, diced
1 small bunch mint, leaves only,
   roughly sliced
120 g crustless stale sourdough bread,
   roughly chopped
1 egg, lightly beaten
salt flakes, to taste
100 g aged Pecorino Sardo, freshly grated

**This recipe (in the photo on page 50) makes a great first course or side dish.
I also love it cold the next day with bread and an extra drizzle of olive oil.**

Trim ends off zucchini and cut in half lengthways. Hollow out each half, leaving enough flesh on all sides to give a shell that is strong enough to hold the filling. Roughly chop the scooped-out zucchini flesh.

Preheat oven to 200°C.

Heat a frying pan over medium heat, add oil and, when hot, shallow-fry zucchini shells, turning as needed, until golden on all sides. Remove from oil and place upside down on paper towel to drain.

Discard all except ¼ cup (60 ml) of the oil from the pan, add garlic and anchovy fillets and cook for a minute. Add chopped zucchini and tomatoes and cook until soft but not coloured, about 5 minutes. Transfer to a food processor, add mint, bread, egg, salt and half the pecorino, and pulse to combine well.

Fill zucchini shells with mixture, mounding it up slightly. Arrange in a single layer in a baking dish and carefully sprinkle the top of each zucchini with remaining pecorino. Cook in oven for about 20 minutes until cheese is golden.

Serve with a drizzle of olive oil.

Stuffed Vegetables

The popularity of stuffed vegetables in Sardinia is one of many examples of Arabic influence. Typically the centre of vegetables such as zucchini or eggplant is scooped out and mixed with coarse breadcrumbs, egg and seasoning, put back into the vegetable shell, then baked with a little tomato sauce; rice is also a popular stuffing, especially for tomatoes. I like to serve a selection of different stuffed vegetables as an antipasto.

VEAL-STUFFED EGGPLANT

MELANZANE RIPIENE

Left: Veal-stuffed Eggplant (this page);
right: Stuffed Zucchini (page 49)

SERVES 8 AS A FIRST COURSE

4 eggplants (aubergines), halved
   lengthways
salt flakes and freshly ground black
   pepper, to taste
½ cup (125 ml) extra virgin olive oil,
   plus extra for frying and drizzling
2 cloves garlic, peeled and bruised
4 thick slices stale ciabatta, crusts
   removed, roughly chopped
2 tablespoons flat-leaf parsley leaves
200 g veal mince
200 g pork mince
100 g flat pancetta, finely chopped
80 g aged Pecorino Sardo, freshly grated,
   plus extra for sprinkling
4 eggs, lightly beaten
600 ml Passata (see page 218)

This recipe is based on one my mother-in-law, Rosalia, cooks; she's from Abruzzo, but it's very similar to the way my mother would prepare eggplants in Sardinia. They are delicious as a first course or side dish. I also love them cold the next day, either as they are or on a *panino*.

Scoop eggplant flesh out of the skin, leaving a 1 cm thick shell. Sprinkle shell with salt and set aside, upside down, to drain a little. Meanwhile, chop eggplant flesh. Heat a frying pan over medium heat, add oil and, when hot, add eggplant flesh and 1 garlic clove and cook for about 10 minutes, until eggplant is soft and lightly coloured. Remove garlic clove.

Place ciabatta, parsley and remaining garlic clove in a food processor and process until combined. Transfer to a large bowl, add veal and pork mince, pancetta, cooked eggplant, pecorino, egg, salt and pepper and mix well to combine. If it seems a little dry, add some extra oil.

Preheat oven to 180°C.

Pat eggplant shells dry, then fill with mince mixture, mounding it up slightly. Heat a frying pan over medium heat, add a little oil and, when hot, add the stuffed eggplants, filling-side down. Fry for about 5 minutes, until golden, then turn and cook other side for 3–4 minutes until soft.

Coat the base of a baking dish with some of the passata. Arrange eggplants in it in a single layer and pour the remaining passata over the top. Cover tightly with a double layer of foil (see page 222) and cook in oven for about 30 minutes, until a wooden skewer can be inserted into the eggplant shells without any resistance.

Remove from oven and turn on overhead grill. Remove foil, sprinkle tops of eggplants with extra pecorino and grill for a few minutes to brown the cheese. Serve drizzled with a little olive oil.

STUFFED ARTICHOKES

CARCIOFI RIPIENI

SERVES 6 AS A FIRST COURSE

1 lemon, halved
12 globe artichokes
100 ml extra virgin olive oil,
   plus extra for drizzling
200 ml Vermentino (see page 219)
   or other dry white wine

STUFFING

20 g prosciutto
20 g flat pancetta
20 g guanciale (see page 220)
20 g capocollo
20 g sopressa
1 small brown onion, roughly chopped
2 cloves garlic, sliced
¼ teaspoon dried chilli flakes
100 g crustless stale sourdough bread,
   roughly chopped
1 teaspoon finely chopped rosemary leaves
½ teaspoon thyme leaves
2 tablespoons finely sliced
   flat-leaf parsley leaves
1 egg
30 g parmesan, freshly grated
salt flakes, to taste

At the restaurant we use a mixture of cold cuts for the stuffing, including capocollo (also called coppa) or cured pork neck and sopressa salami, but you can use 100 g of whatever Italian cold cuts you have on hand. Parmesan ranges from the finest Italian Parmigiano Reggiano to the worst, pre-grated, rancid-smelling powders in supermarkets. Try to find a good Parmigiano Reggiano or Grana Padano for this recipe; if unavailable, use an aged Italian pecorino.

To make the stuffing, place prosciutto, pancetta, guanciale, capocollo, sopressa, onion, garlic, chilli, bread, rosemary, thyme and parsley in a food processor and pulse until finely minced. Add egg, parmesan and salt and pulse to combine. Set aside.

Add lemon juice and squeezed lemon halves to a large bowl of cold water. Working with one artichoke at a time, peel off the dark outer leaves until you reach the tender light-green ones. Using a sharp paring knife, cut off the top third of the artichoke. Trim the stalk so that it's just a couple of centimetres long, peel it. Using a teaspoon, scoop any hairy choke out of the centre of the artichoke. Rub the artichoke with one of the lemon halves from the bowl, then place in the acidulated water. Repeat with remaining artichokes.

Drain artichokes upside down on paper towel. Pack stuffing firmly between the leaves and in the centre of each artichoke, mounding it up slightly on the top.

Heat a large saucepan over medium heat, add oil and, when hot, add artichokes, stuffing-side down, and cook for about 5 minutes until the stuffing forms a slight crust. Pour in wine, bring to the boil, reduce heat to lowest setting, cover and simmer for about 20 minutes, until a wooden skewer can be inserted into the base of the artichokes without any resistance.

Remove artichokes from the pan, place onto plates and serve with pan juices and a drizzle of olive oil.

ARTICHOKES WITH POTATOES

CARCIOFI CON PATATE

SERVES 6 AS A FIRST COURSE

1 lemon, halved
6 globe artichokes *or* 12 baby globe
    artichokes
3 spunta potatoes
¼ cup (60 ml) extra virgin olive oil,
    plus extra for drizzling
1 clove garlic, peeled and bruised
handful flat-leaf parsley leaves
⅓ cup (80 ml) Vermentino (see page 219)
    or other dry white wine
1 litre Chicken Stock (see page 214)
salt flakes and freshly ground black
    pepper, to taste

*Above: Artichokes with Potatoes (this page);
below: Grilled Mixed Vegetables (page 61)*

The artichokes that grow in Sardinia have pointy spikes on the tips of their bracts (the petal-like leaves that are eaten) and have a purple tinge; they may be called *spinoso sardo* or spiny artichokes. I remember my mum often making this slow-braised dish, cooking the artichokes and potatoes together in a big heavy pot until they were very soft. I used to love the leftovers squashed into a paste as a filling for a *panino*.

Add lemon juice and squeezed lemon halves to a large bowl of cold water. Working with one artichoke at a time, peel off the dark outer leaves until you reach the tender light-green ones. Using a sharp paring knife, cut off the top third of the artichoke. Trim the stalk so that it's just a couple of centimetres long, peel it. Cut artichokes into quarters (or halves if small) and, using a teaspoon, scoop any hairy choke out of the centre. Rub the cut surfaces with one of the lemon halves from the bowl, then place the artichokes in the acidulated water. Repeat with remaining artichokes.

Peel potatoes and cut into pieces the same size as the artichokes.

Heat a saucepan over medium heat, add oil and, when hot, add garlic and parsley, then cook for a few minutes until garlic is lightly coloured. Add artichoke and potato and cook for 3 minutes, stirring occasionally. Add wine, increase heat and cook for a minute or two until it starts to boil. Add stock, salt and pepper and bring back to the boil, then reduce heat and simmer for 30 minutes, occasionally stirring gently so as not to break up the potatoes.

Drizzle with olive oil, sprinkle with salt and pepper and serve.

BROAD BEANS WITH CURED PORK CHEEK

FAVE E GUANCIALE

SERVES 6–8 AS PART
OF AN ANTIPASTO

2 tablespoons extra virgin olive oil
1 salad onion, finely diced
1 sprig rosemary, leaves picked
   and very finely chopped
1 × 150 g piece guanciale (see page 220),
   diced
2 kg young broad beans in pods, shelled
salt flakes and freshly ground black
   pepper, to taste
½ cup (125 ml) Vermentino (see page 219)
   or other dry white wine

You'll often see this dish as an antipasto at an *agriturismo* (farm guesthouse) when broad beans are in season. When the first baby broad beans of the season (called *fave novelle*, literally 'new beans') appear they are the size of a green bean and you don't peel them at all as the beans themselves are so tiny that you can cook the whole pod. In Padru, the town near my parents' village, there's a shop called *frutta e verdure* ('fruit and vegetables'); you go into the shop, walk beyond into the field, pick the fruit and vegetables that you want, then take them back into the shop to weigh and pay. This is where my parents buy broad beans, tomatoes, chicory and whatever else is in season.

Heat a frying pan over low heat, add oil and, when hot, add onion and cook for a couple of minutes, until soft but not coloured. Add rosemary and guanciale and cook for a further 8–10 minutes, until the fat in the guanciale has melted. Stir through broad beans and a little salt. Add wine, increase heat and cook until wine evaporates. Add 1 cup (250 ml) of water, bring to the boil, then reduce heat and simmer for 20 minutes, stirring occasionally. If it dries out and the beans start to stick, add another tablespoon or two of water.

Add salt and a good grind of pepper and serve hot or at room temperature.

Note

Mature broad beans need to be double-peeled: taken out of their long pod and then the tough outer skin removed from each bean; however, if they are young and tender enough, as they should be for this recipe, just take them out of the long pod and leave the outer skin on.

BORLOTTI BEAN, TUSCAN CABBAGE AND FREGOLONE SOUP

MINESTRA DI BORLOTTI, CAVOLO NERO E FREGOLONE

SERVES 6 AS A FIRST COURSE

600 g fresh borlotti beans in pods, shelled

100 g desiree potato (about 1 small potato), peeled

50 ml extra virgin olive oil, plus extra for drizzling

1 clove garlic, finely sliced

1 small brown onion, finely diced

1 carrot, peeled and finely diced

1 stalk celery heart, finely diced

2 sprigs thyme

3 bay leaves

1 small sprig rosemary

400 g canned peeled tomatoes, drained and squashed

salt flakes and freshly ground black pepper, to taste

fine sea salt, for pasta water

200 g fregolone (see page 106)

½ bunch cavolo nero, stems discarded, leaves roughly chopped

finely grated zest of 1 lemon

crusty bread, for serving

Legumes, such as borlotti beans, lentils and chickpeas, need to be cooked over very low heat otherwise they'll be tough. It's also important to rest dishes such as soups before serving them; when I take a pot of soup off the heat to rest it, I partially cover it so the steam can still escape. Cavolo nero (sometimes called Tuscan cabbage), is a member of the cabbage family with thick, curly dark green leaves. It is becoming more widely available in greengrocers.

Place borlotti beans and potato in a saucepan, add enough water to just cover. Bring to the boil, reduce heat to lowest setting and simmer for 25 minutes. Drain, reserving cooking liquid. Crush potato with a little of the cooking liquid. Set aside.

Heat a large saucepan over high heat, add oil and, when hot, add garlic, onion, carrot and celery and cook for about 8 minutes, until soft and golden. Add beans, thyme, bay leaves and rosemary and cook for a further 2 minutes. Straining off any sediment, add the reserved cooking liquid to the saucepan. Add tomato, potato and salt flakes and bring to the boil then reduce heat and simmer for 15 minutes, skimming regularly to remove any froth that rises to the surface.

Meanwhile, bring a large saucepan of water to the boil, add fine sea salt, then fregolone and boil for 4 minutes. Drain well and add to soup with cavolo nero and lemon zest and cook for a further 10 minutes or so, until cavolo nero is tender.

Remove from heat, add salt and pepper, remove thyme and rosemary stems (if you can find them), partially cover and set aside to rest for 5 minutes.

Serve drizzled with olive oil, with crusty bread on the side.

GREEN BEANS WITH GARLIC AND MINT DRESSING

FAGIOLINI VERDI CON AGLIO E MENTUCCIA

1 tablespoon fine sea salt
80 g Roman beans, tailed and halved on the diagonal
80 g baby green beans, tailed
¼ cup (60 ml) extra virgin olive oil
2 tablespoons finely sliced mint leaves
1 clove garlic, finely sliced
salt flakes and freshly ground black pepper, to taste

Green beans are sold two ways: hand-picked or machine-picked. The hand-picked beans are usually sold in punnets and cost at least twice as much, but they're worth it; often labelled baby beans, they're small, straight and tender. Roman beans, also known as Italian flat beans, are long wide green beans that are eaten pod and all. The quicker you cook green beans the better they'll keep their colour, so it's important to use plenty of water and return it to the boil as quickly as possible. Salt also helps to lock in the colour, and the other trick is to refresh them in iced water as soon as they're cooked – though if you want to serve them hot, skip this step. Shown in the photo on page 82, these beans go particularly well with fish dishes.

Bring 2 litres of water to the boil in a large saucepan, then stir in fine sea salt. Add beans, return to the boil, then cook for 3–4 minutes, until tender. Drain beans and plunge into iced water.

When the beans are cool, drain well, pat dry and toss with oil, mint, garlic, salt flakes and pepper.

Serve at room temperature.

Sardinian Olive Oil

Olive trees have grown wild in Sardinia's dry, rocky soil since time immemorial and their oil was traded around the Mediterranean by Phoenicians, Carthaginians and Romans. Olive cultivation increased with the spread of monasteries and their extensive plantings after 1000 AD and again with Spanish rule in the 15th century, when laws were passed to ensure new trees were grafted and new olive presses built. The House of Savoy, taking over from the Spanish in the early 1700s, continued the expansion, decreeing that olive trees be planted on the boundaries of land.

Since 2007, Sardinian extra virgin olive oil has had PDO (Protected Designation of Origin – DOP in Italian) status within the European Union, which has encouraged small-scale production of quality oil, some of which is organic. Sardegna Extra Virgin Olive Oil DOP is produced in the provinces of Cagliari, Oristano, Nuoro and Sassari (more than half the island) from native olives – mainly Bosane, but also Semidana, Tonda di Cagliari, Nera di Villacidro and up to 14 other minor varieties. Sardinian olive oil has a grassy, fruity aroma, a slight bitterness (which many people compare to artichokes) and a peppery finish. If possible, use it in the dishes in this book for an authentic taste of Sardinia.

RAW VEGETABLE SALAD

INSALATA DI PINZIMONIO

SERVES 4 AS AN ACCOMPANIMENT

2 bulbs baby fennel with fronds
2 carrots, peeled
2 stalks celery heart with leaves
50 ml extra virgin olive oil
juice of ½ lemon, strained
handful flat-leaf parsley leaves,
    finely sliced
salt flakes and freshly ground black
    pepper, to taste

Pinzimonio, the Italian version of French *crudités*, is a Tuscan dish that's also very popular in Sardinia; it's traditionally served as a water glass of raw vegetables with an olive oil and lemon juice dipping sauce on the side. This salad (in the photo on page 118) is a great appetiser as the acid and crunch stimulate the appetite. In this more refined version, I've cut the vegetables into smaller strips and made them into a salad with the dipping sauce as a dressing. It works well as a fresh accompaniment to cut through the richness of roast meats, especially ones that are fatty, like suckling pig, or have a strong flavour (such as lamb or mutton). Baby cos lettuce leaves are often added to a traditional *pinzimonio* and other vegetables, such as globe artichokes, can be added when they're in season.

Separate layers of fennel bulb, wash well, dry, then cut into strips about 5 cm long × 1 cm wide. Roughly chop fennel fronds. Cut carrots and celery stalks into 5 cm × 1 cm strips, reserving celery leaves.

Place fennel bulb, carrot and celery stalk in a bowl. Pour over oil and lemon juice. Add parsley, fennel fronds, celery leaves, salt and pepper and toss to combine well.

GRILLED MIXED VEGETABLES

GRIGLIATA MISTA DI VERDURE

SERVES 4 AS AN ACCOMPANIMENT
OR PART OF AN ANTIPASTO

1 Treviso radicchio
4 female zucchini (courgette) flowers,
    with baby zucchini attached
1 white witlof, trimmed and quartered
1 red witlof, trimmed and quartered
extra virgin olive oil, for drizzling

HERB DRESSING

2 tablespoons finely sliced
    flat-leaf parsley leaves
1 sprig marjoram, leaves picked
½ clove garlic, finely sliced
juice of ½ lemon, strained
⅓ cup (80 ml) extra virgin olive oil
salt flakes, to taste

Lettuces aren't just great served raw in salads. Italians often also cook them, especially the ones with firmer leaves, such as radicchio, endive and witlof. This colourful dish is in the photo on page 54.

Heat a barbecue grill-plate or char-grill pan to medium.

Discard outer leaves of the radicchio until you get to the deep red leaves, then cut into quarters. Remove the stamen from inside each zucchini flower and trim the end off the small zucchini attached. Drizzle all vegetables with oil.

To make the herb dressing, place all ingredients in a blender and blend until well combined.

Grill radicchio and witlof for about 8 minutes, turning as needed to colour all sides. After 4 minutes, add zucchini flowers and grill, turning to colour all sides.

Arrange vegetables on a serving platter, drizzle with some of the herb dressing and serve with remaining dressing on the side.

SALAD of BOTTARGA with SARDINIAN ARTICHOKES

INSALATINA DI BOTTARGA E CARCIOFI SARDI

1 Treviso radicchio
6 marinated Sardinian baby artichokes, quartered
2 bulbs baby fennel, washed well and finely sliced
2 stalks celery heart, finely sliced
1 × 60 g piece bottarga (see page 93), peeled and finely sliced

VINAIGRETTE DRESSING

⅓ cup (80 ml) extra virgin olive oil
2 tablespoons strained lemon juice
salt flakes, to taste

When an artichoke plant produces lots of buds, the farmer will often cut some of them off while they're still small, so the plant's energy can go into growing the remaining buds to full size. These young artichokes don't need to be trimmed and are often just sliced and eaten raw; they're also preserved in oil and exported around the world. If you can't find Sardinian baby artichokes, use the best-quality preserved artichokes you can.

Discard outer leaves of the radicchio until you come to the red leaves, then slice thinly. Combine radicchio, artichoke, fennel and celery in a bowl.

To make the vinaigrette dressing, place all ingredients in a screw-top jar and shake well to emulsify.

Pour just enough dressing over the vegetables to coat them and toss gently. Arrange on a platter and scatter bottarga over the top.

WARM POTATO AND ONION SALAD

INSALATA DI PATATE LESSE E CIPOLLE

SERVES 6 AS AN ACCOMPANIMENT

1 kg spunta potatoes
fine sea salt
¼ cup (60 ml) extra virgin olive oil
3 brown onions, halved, finely sliced
salt flakes and freshly ground black
    pepper, to taste
1 cup (250 ml) Ichnusa beer or other
    lager-style beer
2 sprigs flat-leaf parsley

This is my mum's potato salad (in the photo page 113). I remember eating it often with boiled meats (called *bollito* in Italian) – usually on a Sunday, when we'd have hen (see page 139) or mutton (see page 120). It's also great with Spit-roasted Lamb Offal (see page 135) and roasts, such as Kid Cooked 'Shepherd-style' (see page 112).

Cook the potatoes, in their skins, in boiling salted water for about 30 minutes, until a wooden skewer can be inserted without any resistance. Using a slotted spoon, remove from the water and place in a colander to drain. When cool enough to handle, peel and cut into 1 cm thick slices. Place on a serving platter, overlapping the slices slightly.

Heat a frying pan, add oil and, when hot, add onion and salt. Cook over low–medium heat until well coloured and very soft, about 15 minutes, stirring occasionally. Add beer, increase heat and boil until most of the liquid evaporates, stirring constantly. Add salt and pepper. Pour over the potatoes. Tear parsley leaves over the top and serve.

WINTER SALAD

INSALATA D'INVERNO

SERVES 4 AS AN ACCOMPANIMENT

1 Treviso radicchio
1 baby cos lettuce
1 witlof
2 red radishes

RED WINE VINEGAR DRESSING

2 teaspoons red wine vinegar
2 teaspoons white balsamic condiment
    (see page 221)
¼ cup (60 ml) extra virgin olive oil
1 small golden shallot, finely chopped

Sardinians don't eat a lot of root vegetables, with the exception of radishes (called *rape* in Italian), which are very popular. I remember my father planting, from seed, what he thought were radishes, only to discover when he pulled them up that they were beetroots. He'd never seen a beetroot before and thought they were quite freaky. I had to explain to him that they were *rape rossa*, and that you could eat the leaves as well as the roots. Once I showed him how to cook them, he was converted. I use my father-in-law's homemade red wine vinegar for this dish (in the photo on page 155) – you want one that has a bit of a bite.

Discard the outer leaves of the radicchio until you come to the deep red leaves. Separate remaining leaves and put into a sink of cold water. Discard any soft outer leaves from the baby cos, separate remaining leaves and add to the sink. Separate witlof leaves and add to the sink. Drain and dry leaves and slice them all in half lengthways.

Wash and dry radishes and slice thinly, ideally on a mandoline.

To make the red wine vinegar dressing, place all ingredients in a screw-top jar and shake well to emulsify.

Place radicchio, cos, witlof and radish in a large bowl, pour over just enough dressing to coat and toss well.

CHICORY WITH CITRUS

CICORIA AGLI AGRUMI

SERVES 4 AS AN ACCOMPANIMENT

2 bunches chicory
fine sea salt, for boiling chicory
¼ cup (60 ml) extra virgin olive oil
1 clove garlic, peeled and bruised
salt flakes and freshly ground black
    pepper, to taste
1 lemon, segmented
1 lime, segmented
1 orange, segmented
1 ruby grapefruit, segmented

Chicory belongs to the same family as lettuce, dandelion and many other edible plants. It's cultivated in several forms, including witlof and radicchio, but the type used in this dish resembles the original wild chicory with long white stems and slightly bitter, dark green, spiky leaves that look similar to wild dandelion greens. Other leafy greens, such as cime di rapa, cavolo nero and spinach, can also be prepared this way. This side dish (in the photo on page 146) is a great accompaniment to simple grilled fish, as well as many of the dishes in this book, including Snapper with White Wine, Green Olives and Parsley (see page 83) and Kid Cooked 'Shepherd-style' (see page 112).

Cut the stems off the chicory. Fold each leaf in half and tear out the tough stem, leaving only the last 5 cm or so. Cut leaves, with remaining stem, into 5 cm lengths. Wash well. Bring a large saucepan of water to the boil, add fine sea salt, then chicory and boil for 10–15 minutes, until stem section is tender. Tip into a colander and press to remove excess water.

Heat a frying pan over medium heat, add oil and, when hot, add garlic and cook for a few minutes until golden. Discard garlic. Add chicory, salt flakes and pepper and cook for a couple of minutes, stirring constantly, until chicory is thoroughly coated in oil.

Remove from heat and stir through 5 lemon segments, 5 lime segments, 5 orange segments and 5 grapefruit segments. Serve hot or at room temperature.

Note

To segment citrus fruit, use a small sharp knife to remove the skin and white pith, hold the fruit in the palm of one hand over a bowl and cut down either side of the white membrane, lift the segment out and drop it into the bowl; when you've finished, squeeze the leftovers over the bowl to capture all the juice. You won't need all of the segments for this recipe, but the rest make good snacks or the beginnings of a simple dessert.

BAKED MUSHROOMS WITH BREAD AND CURED PORK CHEEK

FUNGHI AL FORNO CON PANE E GUANCIALE

SERVES 4 AS A FIRST COURSE

12 cup mushrooms

½ cup (125 ml) extra virgin olive oil,
   plus extra for oiling

1 small brown onion, finely diced

80 g guanciale (see page 220), finely diced

2 sprigs marjoram, leaves picked

salt flakes and freshly ground black
   pepper, to taste

2 slices stale ciabatta, roughly chopped

80 g aged Pecorino Sardo, freshly grated

2 teaspoons dried Greek oregano
   (see page 220)

It's important that you don't wash mushrooms, or they'll become waterlogged and slimy; just wipe them gently with a damp cloth. This is also good served with meat, or as part of an antipasto – in which case, this quantity is enough for 12 people.

Preheat oven to 200°C.

Wipe mushrooms over with a clean, damp cloth. Remove and finely chop the stems.

Heat a frying pan over medium heat, add oil and, when hot, add onion and guanciale. Cook for about 3 minutes, until onion is soft and slightly coloured. Stir in mushroom stems, then reduce heat and cook for about 10 minutes, stirring occasionally, until well softened. Stir in marjoram, salt and pepper and remove from the heat.

Lay mushroom caps on an oiled baking tray and fill them with the onion mixture.

Place ciabatta, pecorino, oregano, salt and pepper in a blender and pulse to a fine crumb. Sprinkle over the mushrooms and place in oven for about 10 minutes until lightly coloured.

Serve hot or at room temperature.

Seafood

Until relatively recently, seafood didn't feature strongly in Sardinian cooking, as most of the island's population lived inland in the hills and mountains. Centuries of invasion by foreign powers and pirate raids had taught the people to be wary of the sea and the coast. Foreigners were Sardinia's first real fishermen: Ligurians, who founded the town of Carloforte on the island of San Pietro to fish for tuna, didn't share the Sardinians' suspicion of the sea – and the tuna industry still thrives on this small island southwest of the Sardinian mainland, which hosts an annual tuna festival in May.

It wasn't until the early 1960s, when Prince Karim Aga Khan IV, bought 5000 hectares of land on the northeast coast of the island, naming it the Costa Smeralda ('emerald coast') and developing it into one of Italy's most exclusive and tasteful playgrounds for the super-rich, that the Sardinians began to value their coastline, and seafood became a mainstay, at least of coastal menus. This sudden influx of money came with an interesting twist: as the land along the coast was 'good for nothing' as far as traditional wisdom was concerned, it was often owned by women, the males of the family having inherited the more valuable grazing and farming land in the interior. As a result, there were some very wealthy women in Sardinia by the time the Aga Khan and his friends had finished their buying spree along the Costa Smeralda.

The harvest from the island's 1800 kilometres of coastline has become increasingly popular over the past 50 years. Typical of Mediterranean cuisine, ingredients with strong flavours, such as bottarga (dried mullet roe; see page 93) and sardines, are prized. Most seafood dishes are prepared quite simply, so as not to overshadow the flavour of the seafood. Fish are generally cooked whole (sometimes gut-in and unscaled), lightly seasoned with salt, olive oil and lemon juice, and are often grilled over coals (see page 84). Small, inexpensive fish, including sardines, grey mullet, bream, scorpionfish, whiting and red mullet, are among the most popular. Fish cooked on the bone tastes best, but if you prefer to cook fillets, at least leave the skin on as the fat between the skin and flesh adds flavour. *Crudo* (raw seafood) is now also very popular along the coast, especially in the capital city of Cagliari. It's important to take all fish out of the fridge about 30 minutes or so before cooking, to allow it to come to room temperature. If serving it raw, make sure you buy the freshest fish possible – sashimi-grade – and serve it at room temperature.

Small shellfish, such as mussels, limpets, sea urchins, tiny crabs and clams, are harvested from the rocks and beaches, while mussels and oysters are farmed in the Gulf of Olbia in the northeast, where a mussel festival is held every year. The port town of Alghero, on the west coast, which was invaded by Catalans a thousand years ago, is famed for its lobsters. Unlike the lobsters of the North Atlantic, with their large front claws, these lobsters, sometimes called spiny lobsters, have much smaller front pincers. Octopus, squid and cuttlefish are found all around Sardinia's rocky coast and are common in soups, ragùs and braises, with the ink from the cuttlefish often used to colour pasta and risotto.

See also
- Malloreddus with Clams, Bottarga and Zucchini Flowers (page 20) in 'Pasta and Rice'
- Lemon Taglierini with Sea Urchin and Artichoke Cream (page 26) in 'Pasta and Rice'
- Trofie Pasta Carloforte-style (page 29) in 'Pasta and Rice'
- Fusilli with Squid and Saffron Sauce (page 30) in 'Pasta and Rice'
- Hand-rolled Macaroni with Crab and Grape Tomatoes (page 32) in 'Pasta and Rice'
- Lombrichi Pasta with Octopus Sauce (page 34) in 'Pasta and Rice'
- Fregola Cooked Risotto-style with Seafood Sauce (page 38) in 'Pasta and Rice'
- Salad of Bottarga with Sardinian Artichokes (page 62) in 'Vegetables'
- Trout with White Wine and Rosemary (page 158) in 'Hunting and Foraging'
- Tonnarelli Pasta with Smoked Eel and Squid (page 161) in 'Hunting and Foraging'

RED MULLET FILLETS WITH ZUCCHINI, TOMATO AND PECORINO

FILETTI DI TRIGLIE ALLA SARDA

SERVES 4

8 × 90 g red mullet fillets, skin on

plain flour, for dusting

extra virgin olive oil, for pan-frying

1 small brown onion, finely sliced

1 small yellow zucchini (courgette),
   finely sliced

1 small green zucchini (courgette),
   finely sliced

1 clove garlic, finely sliced

2 roma (plum) tomatoes, tops cut off,
   seeded and diced

salt flakes, to taste

50 g young Pecorino Sardo, freshly grated

In most of Italy, you rarely see cheese served with fish, but in Sardinia it's not uncommon to serve young pecorino with seafood; this classic dish is one example. Red mullet are very popular in the Mediterranean, but john dory or whiting would also be great prepared this way.

Remove fish fillets from the fridge 20 minutes before cooking. Using a pair of fish tweezers, remove any small bones from the fillets, then cover and set aside in a cool place to come to room temperature.

Working in batches if necessary, dust fish fillets lightly with flour, shaking off any excess. Heat a frying pan over medium heat, add a little oil and, when hot, cook fillets skin-side down until almost cooked through; press down gently with an egg lifter or fish slice to stop them from curling. Turn and cook on the other side for a few seconds, then remove from pan and set aside.

Add onion to the same pan and fry until soft and lightly coloured. Add zucchini, garlic, tomato and salt and cook for a further 2 minutes. Place fish fillets on top of zucchini and tomato, sprinkle with grated pecorino and cover for a minute until cheese melts. Serve immediately.

CRUMBED SARDINES WITH PECORINO AND EGGPLANT PUREE

SARDINE CON PECORINO SARDO E SALSA DI MELANZANE

SERVES 6 AS A FIRST COURSE

100 g wild rocket, washed and dried
extra virgin olive oil, for dressing rocket and frying sardines
juice of 1 lemon, strained
salt flakes and freshly ground black pepper, to taste
plain flour, for coating sardines
3 eggs, lightly beaten
3 cups (210 g) fine fresh breadcrumbs
18 small butterflied sardines
150 g young Pecorino Sardo, freshly grated

EGGPLANT PURÉE

3 large eggplants (aubergines)
1 clove garlic, peeled
1 tablespoon finely sliced flat-leaf parsley leaves
salt flakes and freshly ground black pepper, to taste
juice of ½ lemon, strained
90 ml extra virgin olive oil

It's tempting to speculate that the name of these small fish is related to the island of Sardinia, though this cannot be proven. Regardless, they are abundant throughout the Mediterranean and are popular in Sardinian cooking. Some eggplants are seedless, but if the ones you're using have visible seeds, scoop them out with a teaspoon to make sure you get a smooth purée.

For eggplant purée, preheat oven to 200°C. Place whole eggplants in oven for 35–45 minutes, until very soft. As soon as they're cool enough to handle, peel and remove seeds if necessary. Process the eggplant flesh in a blender with garlic, parsley, salt, pepper and lemon juice, then, with the machine running, drizzle in enough oil to create a smooth consistency; you may not need it all.

Toss rocket with oil, lemon juice, salt and pepper and set aside.

Arrange three shallow bowls on your workbench: place flour in one, beaten egg in another, and breadcrumbs in the last one. Check sardines for bones, pull off back fins and trim off the belly flaps. Place sardines skin-side down on a clean, dry workbench. Place some pecorino on half of each sardine and fold over to enclose. Roll sardines in flour, dip in egg, then coat in breadcrumbs.

Heat a large frying pan over medium heat, add oil and, when hot, cook sardines until lightly golden.

Place 3 sardines on each plate, sprinkle with salt and serve with rocket and eggplant purée on the side.

Note
Make fresh breadcrumbs by pulsing stale bread in a food processor until finely crumbed.

JOHN DORY FILLETS WITH CLAMS AND ARTICHOKES

FILETTI DI SAN PIETRO CON VONGOLE E CARCIOFI

SERVES 4

4 × 180 g john dory fillets, skin on
1 lemon, halved
4 globe artichokes *or* 8 baby globe
   artichokes
1 teaspoon fine sea salt
¼ teaspoon saffron threads
50 g butter
⅓ cup (80 ml) extra virgin olive oil
2 sprigs marjoram, leaves picked
freshly ground black pepper, to taste

STEAMED VONGOLE

¼ cup (60 ml) extra virgin olive oil
2 cloves garlic, peeled and bruised
500 g vongole (clams), purged
   (see page 221)
½ cup (125 ml) Fish Stock (see page 213)

John dory is normally sold with the skin on, so the dark skin marking that distinguishes it from less expensive members of the dory family is visible. Legend has it that this mark is the thumb print of St Peter the fisherman, giving this highly prized fish its Italian name of *pesce San Pietro*. The skin also helps to hold the flesh together during cooking.

Remove fish fillets from the fridge 20 minutes before cooking. Trim off the thin edges of the fillets, cover and set aside in a cool place to come to room temperature.

For the steamed vongole, heat a frying pan over high heat, add oil and, when hot, add garlic and cook for a minute. Add vongole and stock, cover, shake pan well and cook for a minute or two, until most of the shells open. Remove from heat. Fish out any vongole that haven't opened and, using a blunt knife such as a butter knife, gently prise them open: if the meat is plump and intact on one side of the shell, use them; otherwise discard them. Strain cooking juices, add vongole and set aside.

Add lemon juice and squeezed lemon halves to a large saucepan of cold water. Working with one artichoke at a time, peel off the dark outer leaves until you reach the tender light-green ones. Using a sharp paring knife, cut off the top third of the artichoke. Trim the stalk so that it's just a couple of centimetres long, then peel it. Using a teaspoon, scoop any hairy choke out of the centre of the artichoke. Rub the artichoke with one of the lemon halves from the pan, then place in the acidulated water. Repeat with remaining artichokes. Add salt and cover with a layer of baking paper. Bring to the boil, then reduce heat and simmer for about 15 minutes, until a wooden skewer can be inserted into the base of the artichokes without any resistance. Remove from the water, and, when cool enough to handle, cut artichokes into quarters (or halves, if small) and set aside.

Place vongole and their cooking liquid in a saucepan with the saffron and heat over low heat for 2 minutes. Add artichokes and cook for a further 2 minutes. Set aside to keep warm.

Heat a frying pan over medium heat, add butter and half the oil. When it starts to sizzle, add the fish, skin-side down, and cook for about 4 minutes, until lightly golden and cooked all the way through.

Divide vongole, artichokes and sauce between four warmed plates. Using a spatula or fish slice, transfer fish fillets to plates, placing them on top of the vongole mixture. Sprinkle with marjoram, grind over some pepper and drizzle with remaining oil.

SCORPIONFISH FILLETS WITH SLOW-COOKED RED CAPSICUM AND MUSSELS

FILETTI DI SCORFANO CON PEPERONI BRASATI E COZZE

SERVES 6

18 × 60 g scorpionfish fillets, skin on
⅓ cup (80 ml) extra virgin olive oil
½ brown onion, roughly chopped
1 stalk celery heart, roughly chopped
1 small bunch flat-leaf parsley, stalks only
1 clove garlic, peeled and halved
1.5 kg blue mussels, scrubbed lightly
    with a scourer
300 ml Vermentino (see page 219)
    or other dry white wine
1 tablespoon white balsamic condiment
    (see page 221)
1 tablespoon finely sliced flat-leaf
    parsley leaves
6 sprigs rosemary

SLOW-COOKED RED CAPSICUM

100 ml extra virgin olive oil
3 cloves garlic, finely sliced
1 sprig rosemary, leaves picked
6 red capsicums (peppers), peeled,
    seeded and finely sliced

Scorpionfish is sometimes sold as rockcod or coral perch, and is one of the small, ugly fish that are considered essential in Mediterranean countries for a good seafood stew or hearty soup, such as the French bouillabaisse.

Remove fillets from the fridge 20 minutes before cooking. Remove any small bones from the fillets using a pair of fish tweezers, cover and set aside in a cool place to come to room temperature.

Heat a large frying pan over medium heat, add half the oil and, when hot, add onion, celery, parsley stalks and garlic and cook for a few minutes, until soft but not coloured. Increase heat to high, stir through mussels, then add wine. Cover, shake pan well and cook for about 3 minutes, shaking occasionally, until most of the shells open. Remove from heat. Fish out any mussels haven't opened and, using a blunt knife such as a butter knife, gently prise them open: if the meat is plump and intact on one side of the shell, use them; otherwise discard them. Strain cooking juices and return to the pan. Boil until reduced a little, then set aside. Remove mussel meat from shells, pull off 'beards' and return meat to the pan.

For slow-cooked red capsicum, heat a frying pan over low–medium heat, add oil and, when hot, add garlic and rosemary and cook until garlic softens and begins to colour. Stir in capsicum, reduce heat to as low as possible, cover and cook for 15–20 minutes, stirring occasionally, until soft.

Add mussels, with their cooking liquid, to capsicum mixture and cook for a further 2 minutes. Add white balsamic condiment, parsley leaves and remaining oil. Set aside.

Place fish fillets in a bamboo steamer over a saucepan or wok of boiling water and cook for 6–8 minutes, until just cooked through; a wooden skewer should be able to be inserted without any resistance.

Place mussels and capsicum in a shallow serving bowl, top with fish and pour remaining liquid from capsicum and mussel mixture over the top. Garnish with rosemary.

MULLET BAKED IN A SALT CRUST

MUGGINE AL SALE

SERVES 4

2 × 750–850 g mullet, gilled, gutted and scaled
4 egg whites
3 kg rock salt
olive oil, for oiling

MINT DRESSING

½ cup (125 ml) extra virgin olive oil
2 tablespoons strained lemon juice
2 tablespoons finely sliced mint leaves

We eat a lot of mullet in Sardinia, as their roe is harvested for bottarga, and cooking the fish under a salt crust or *al cartoccio* ('in a paper parcel') are among the most common ways of preparing them. These methods work well because they keep the fish moist and, despite their high oil content, they do have a tendency to dry out. I think mullet's a delicious fish but it needs to be cooked properly or it becomes tough and inedible; if you aren't a fan of strongly flavoured fish, try this dish with bream or snapper instead. Either way, the fish looks and smells fabulous served at the table in its salt crust. You could serve a salad, such as Winter Salad (see page 64) or Green Beans with Garlic and Mint Dressing (see page 60) alongside.

Remove mullet from fridge 30 minutes before cooking. Using a pair of kitchen scissors, cut off fins and trim tails. Thoroughly rinse belly cavities, removing any blood and the black lining from the belly, then pat dry inside and out. Cover and set aside in a cool place to come to room temperature.

Preheat oven to 180°C.

Whisk egg whites until just frothy, not firm. Add salt and mix well.

Place fish on a large, well-oiled baking tray, with some distance between each fish and between the fish and the edges of the tray. Cover the top and the sides of each fish with the salt mixture, packing it firmly around each one to form a layer about 1 cm thick.

Cook in oven for about 35 minutes, until salt starts to get a golden tinge.

Meanwhile, make the mint dressing: place all ingredients in a screw-top jar and shake well to emulsify.

Remove fish from oven and set aside to rest for 5 minutes. Using two spatulas or fish slices, carefully lift fish onto a platter, keeping the salt crust intact.

At the table, crack the salt crust with a small kitchen mallet, lift the pieces of crust away, and let people help themselves to the deliciously moist fish beneath. Shake mint dressing again and serve on the side, for drizzling over the fish.

SNAPPER WITH WHITE WINE, GREEN OLIVES AND PARSLEY

DENTICE ALLA VERNACCIA

SERVES 6

1 × 3 kg snapper, gilled, gutted and scaled
salt flakes, to taste
1 cup (250 ml) extra virgin olive oil
2 cups (500 ml) Fish Stock (see page 213)
4 cloves garlic, finely sliced
30 Bosane olives (see page 219),
  cheeks cut from the pit
2 cups (500 ml) Vernaccia di Oristano
  (see page 219) or other dry white wine
150 g butter, diced
small handful finely sliced
  flat-leaf parsley leaves

In Sardinia we traditionally cook fish whole. I think it has more flavour cooked this way, it looks beautiful sitting on a platter in the centre of the table, and is not as tricky to serve as you might imagine: just use a tablespoon and fork to break off sections of the fish where it has been scored. When all the fish from one side has been eaten, grasp the head and peel it back towards the tail to remove the skeleton, exposing the flesh on the other side. Snapper is a good fish to eat whole, because there aren't many small bones, just lots of lovely moist, sweet flesh. The cheek meat on a large fish like this is a delicacy; when I serve this at home, my son Martino and daughter Sofia always fight over the cheeks. Green Beans with Garlic and Mint Dressing (as in the photo here; see page 60) makes a perfect accompaniment.

Remove snapper from fridge 30–40 minutes before cooking. Cover and set aside in a cool place to come to room temperature.

Using a pair of kitchen scissors, trim fins and tail. Thoroughly rinse belly cavity, removing any blood, then pat dry inside and out. Score snapper on one side, making 5 or 6 diagonal cuts just through to the bone. Sprinkle both sides of the fish generously with salt, patting it into the skin.

Preheat oven to 220°C.

Heat a large heavy-based roasting tin on the stovetop over medium heat. Pour in oil and, when hot, carefully place fish in tin, scored-side down. Cook for about 6 minutes, until skin is crisp, then turn and cook for a further 4 minutes.

Meanwhile, place stock in a small saucepan and bring to the boil. Remove from heat and cover to keep warm.

Scatter garlic and olives over fish, add wine and bring to the boil. Add hot fish stock, cover tightly with a double layer of foil (see page 222) and cook in oven for about 25 minutes, until fish is cooked through, basting frequently. Check the flesh where the fish is scored: the flesh near the bone at the thickest part of the fish should be white.

Remove from oven, place fish on a platter, then cover loosely with foil and set aside in a warm place while you make the sauce.

Place roasting tin on stovetop over high heat, bring cooking juices to the boil and boil until reduced by a third. Whisk in the butter. Stir in parsley and spoon sauce over the fish.

BREAM COOKED OVER THE COALS

ORATA ALLA BRACE

SERVES 4

4 × 500 g bream, gilled, gutted and scaled
5 sprigs rosemary
5 sprigs thyme
150 ml extra virgin olive oil, plus extra
   for drizzling
juice of 2 lemons, strained
1 clove garlic, finely sliced
salt flakes and freshly ground black
   pepper, to taste
crusty bread, for serving
1 clove garlic, peeled and bruised

When my wife Marilyn and I first met, we worked a summer together in a coastal restaurant in Sardinia that specialised in cooking over the coals (*alla brace*). Although this isn't so common in restaurants anymore, people still cook this way at home, making a small fire using just a couple of bricks as a base and building up dry, untreated wood in the centre; acorn is a popular wood for this, as are the roots of the *corbezzolo* ('wild strawberry') tree. This is a perfect dish to cook over a campfire on holidays – wait for the fire to die down to just glowing coals then spread them out a little and cook the fish over them. If an open fire is impractical, you can always use a kettle barbecue. Winter Salad (see page 64) or Warm Potato and Onion Salad (see page 64) would be a perfect accompaniment.

Prepare a fire using dry, untreated wood and allow it to die down to embers.

Meanwhile, remove bream from fridge 30 minutes before cooking. Thoroughly rinse belly cavities, removing any blood, then pat dry inside and out. Cover and set aside in a cool place to come to room temperature.

When fire is ready, place a raised rack over the coals.

Tie rosemary and thyme sprigs together with kitchen string to make a brush. Combine oil, lemon juice, sliced garlic, salt and pepper in a small bowl. Dip herb brush into the oil mixture and brush all over the fish.

Place fish on rack and cook for 6 minutes, basting regularly with the oil mixture. Turn fish over and continue cooking and basting for another 6 minutes or so, until the dorsal (top) fin comes away without offering any resistance. Carefully transfer fish to a serving platter, then cover loosely with foil and set aside to rest for 5 minutes.

Meanwhile, slice bread and grill over the coals. Rub with bruised garlic and drizzle with olive oil.

Serve fish drizzled with a little of the remaining oil mixture, with grilled bread on the side.

TUNA ESCABECHE

TONNO A SCAPECE

SERVES 6 AS A FIRST COURSE

6 × 160 g tuna steaks
⅓ cup (80 ml) extra virgin olive oil
2 cloves garlic, peeled and bruised
500 g roma (plum) tomatoes, tops cut off,
    quartered and seeded
salt flakes and freshly ground white
    pepper, to taste
1½ cups (375 ml) white wine vinegar
3 bay leaves
vegetable oil, for deep-frying
100 g coarse semolina (see page 221)
crusty bread, to serve

This dish, a variation on the Spanish escabeche, is cooked all over Sardinia, though it's most common in Cagliari and Oristano, the two main fishing areas. Traditionally prepared and served in terracotta dishes, it can be made with tomatoes (*in rosso*) or without (*in bianco*). Any oily fish can be used, including mullet, mackerel, yellowtail kingfish and sardines, but tuna works particularly well if you don't have the time to leave the fish to marinate for 12–24 hours, as it tastes great even after just a couple of hours in the marinade.

Remove tuna from fridge 20 minutes before cooking. Cover and set aside in a cool place to come to room temperature.

Heat a frying pan over medium heat, add olive oil and, when hot, add garlic and cook until soft but not coloured. Add tomatoes and salt and pepper, then reduce heat to low and simmer for about 10 minutes, crushing tomatoes with a wooden spoon, until pulpy. Add vinegar and bay leaves, bring to the boil, then reduce heat to medium and cook for a further 5 minutes.

Meanwhile, heat vegetable oil to 160°C (if you don't have a deep-frying thermometer, test the temperature of the oil by dipping the handle of a wooden spoon into it – when bubbles form around the spoon, the oil is hot enough).

Slice each tuna steak, across the grain, into 4–5 strips and dust with semolina. Lower carefully into hot oil and deep-fry for about 2 minutes, until underside is coloured, then turn and fry other side for a further 2 minutes or so, until tuna is cooked through. Set aside on paper towel to drain.

Place tuna in a shallow glass or ceramic dish, pour over the tomato mixture, set aside to cool then cover and refrigerate for between 2 and 24 hours – the longer, the better. If the fish is not fully covered by the marinade, turn it occasionally so that all of it spends time in contact with the marinade.

Serve, in a terracotta dish if possible, with lots of crusty bread to soak up the marinade.

BOTTARGA-CRUSTED TUNA WITH ASPARAGUS

CRUDO DI TONNO IN CROSTA DI BOTTARGA CON ASPARAGI

I often see 'carpaccio' of raw seafood on restaurant menus. Strictly speaking, though, carpaccio was a dish invented at Harry's Bar in Venice in 1950, which consisted of raw beef drizzled with a lemony mayonnaise; it was named for the brilliant reds and whites common in the paintings of Renaissance artist Vittore Carpaccio, who was exhibiting in Venice at the time. In Italy, dishes of raw seafood are generally called *crudo*, which is Italian for 'raw'.

SERVES 4 AS A FIRST COURSE

1 × 350 g piece mid-cut loin
  sashimi-grade tuna
100 g bottarga (see page 93),
  freshly grated and sifted
salt flakes and freshly ground black
  pepper, to taste
⅓ cup (80 ml) extra virgin olive oil
8 green asparagus spears, trimmed
100 g baby mesclun salad leaves,
  washed and dried

SWEET VINEGAR DRESSING

2 tablespoons aged sweet vinegar
⅓ cup (80 ml) extra virgin olive oil
salt flakes and freshly ground black
  pepper, to taste

Top: Raw Scallops with Bottarga (page 91); middle: Cured Swordfish (page 90); bottom: Bottarga-crusted Tuna with Asparagus (this page)

Remove tuna from fridge 30 minutes before cooking. Cover and set aside in a cool place to come to room temperature.

Combine bottarga with salt and pepper, then roll the tuna in this mixture to form a crust. Heat a frying pan, add half the oil and, when hot, add tuna and sear lightly on all sides. Transfer tuna to a plate and place in fridge.

Heat a barbecue grill-plate or char-grill pan. Brush asparagus with remaining oil and grill until well-coloured on all sides. Cut each spear in half on the diagonal.

To make sweet vinegar dressing, place all ingredients in a screw-top jar and shake well to emulsify.

Toss mesclun and asparagus with just enough dressing to coat. Set aside.

Using a sharp knife, cut tuna into 8 slices.

Arrange mesclun, asparagus and tuna on a serving plate and drizzle with remaining dressing.

CURED SWORDFISH

PESCE SPADA MARINATO

SERVES 4 AS A FIRST COURSE

1 x 250 g piece sashimi-grade swordfish
   belly, skinned and bloodline removed
¼ ruby or regular grapefruit, segmented
1 red radish, halved and finely sliced
¼ punnet baby watercress, snipped
salt flakes and freshly ground black
   pepper, to taste

CURING MIXTURE

¼ cup (55 g) castor sugar
¼ cup (55 g) fine sea salt
finely grated zest of 1 lemon
finely grated zest of ½ orange
¼ bunch dill, leaves picked and finely sliced

WHITE BALSAMIC DRESSING

½ small golden shallot, finely chopped
2 teaspoons white balsamic condiment
   (see page 221)
2 tablespoons extra virgin olive oil

Swordfish is a popular fish in the Mediterranean. Its high oil content gives it a lovely texture when served raw, and also makes it a perfect fish for curing. You'll need to start this recipe (in the photo on page 88) a day ahead to give the fish time to cure. The fish needs to be a maximum of 3 cm thick; if it is thicker than this, halve it horizontally or the curing mixture won't penetrate fully.

To make curing mixture, combine all ingredients in a bowl. Place a layer of curing mixture in a glass or ceramic dish. Place fish on top and rub more mixture all over, packing curing mixture on top and around the sides of the fish. Cover and refrigerate for 24 hours, turning fish every 6–8 hours.

Next make the white balsamic dressing. Place all ingredients in a screw-top jar and shake well to emulsify.

Remove fish from dish and wipe down well with a clean, damp Chux or J-Cloth to remove all traces of curing mixture. Cut fish into slices about 2 mm thick. Cut each grapefruit segment into 2 or 3 pieces, depending on size.

Arrange fish on four plates, twisting each slice slightly so that it sits up on the plate. Place radish slices on top of the fish and scatter grapefruit around the plates. Sprinkle with salt, drizzle dressing over the fish and around the plates and scatter baby watercress over the top. Add a grind of pepper and serve.

RAW SCALLOPS WITH BOTTARGA

CRUDO DI CAPESANTE CON BOTTARGA

SERVES 4 AS A FIRST COURSE

pane carasau (see page 6), for serving
extra virgin olive oil, for drizzling
salt flakes and freshly ground black
   pepper, to taste
12 sashimi-grade saucer scallops, trimmed
juice of ½ lemon, strained
1 stalk celery heart, finely sliced
1 bulb baby fennel, washed well
   and finely sliced
1 × 80 g piece bottarga (see page 93),
   peeled and thinly shaved

The saltiness of the bottarga in this dish (in the photo on page 88) enhances the sweetness of the scallops. The celery and fennel add a lovely contrasting crunch. You'll need to buy very fresh, dry scallops for this dish; if they've been frozen or sitting in water, it won't work.

Preheat oven to 200°C.

Drizzle pane carasau with oil, sprinkle with salt flakes, wrap in foil and place in oven for about 5 minutes, until warm.

Meanwhile, slice scallops horizontally in three. Arrange in a single layer on four plates and cover with plastic wrap. Using a small kitchen mallet, gently flatten scallops. Remove plastic wrap and drizzle scallops generously with oil and a little lemon juice.

Arrange celery and fennel on top of the scallops, sprinkle with salt and pepper and scatter bottarga over the top. Drizzle with a little more oil and serve with pane carasau.

BOTTARGA

As inland dwellers, Sardinians needed to preserve the seafood that was caught, making it both portable and durable. *Bottarga di muggine* (sometimes written *buttariga*), the salted, pressed and air-dried roe sac of grey mullet, has been made on the island for over 3000 years. In fact bottarga has been produced all over the Mediterranean since ancient times. The Greeks call it *avgotaraho*, the French *poutargue*, in Spain it's *botarga* and in Arabic, *batarekh*. Tuna roe (*bottarga di tonno*), which is cured in a similar way, has a stronger flavour and is more popular in North Africa.

From August to October the female grey mullets are full of roe, which is carefully extracted so as not to break the sac, then salted, pressed between wooden paddles and dried for a month or more, during which time it is rubbed regularly to get rid of any air pockets between the roe and the sac. Traditionally it was hung on hooks by the end of the sac in a cool, dry place and air-dried, then sealed in beeswax to preserve it. When I was working in my Zio (Uncle) Elio's bar in Olbia, almost 30 years ago, I remember the fishermen would give him gifts of bottarga dipped in beeswax. The adults loved it and I hated it – I guess it's an acquired taste, because now I love it too. These days the roe is still salted and pressed, but now it's dried on perforated trays in a special temperature-controlled room, then cryovaced; I haven't seen beeswax-coated bottarga for years. The roe is dried for at least 1 month, when it's great for slicing, but if it's going to be used for grating it should be aged for 3–4 months.

When I realised that most Sardinian bottarga was made with imported roe – including roe from Australia – I thought why send roe to Sardinia to be turned into bottarga that's sold back to us in Australia? So I started looking around for someone who could produce it locally. I came across a Sardinian guy in Queensland, Massimo Scala, who produces *salumi*. Together we sourced Australian mullet roe and now he produces bottarga for me, as well as a range of Sardinian-style *salumi*: see page 219 for details of where to buy bottarga.

Bottarga looks like a flat orange sausage and is Sardinia's favourite seasoning. It is eaten grated over pasta, shaved over salad, or on its own with crusty bread and a glass of wine. You can feel through the cryovac packaging to check if it's a nice soft one for slicing or a firmer one for grating. If slicing bottarga, peel it first. But if grating, leave the membrane on to help hold the piece together: some of the membrane will flake away as you grate and can easily be discarded; sift the grated bottarga to remove the rest.

DEEP-FRIED SEAFOOD AND VEGETABLES WITH CHILLI MAYONNAISE

PICCOLO FRITTO MISTO DI PESCE E VERDURE CON MAIONESE AL PEPERONCINO

SERVES 6 AS A FIRST COURSE

3 × 120 g squid, cleaned and skinned
6 female zucchini (courgette) flowers,
    with baby zucchini attached
150 g plain flour
150 g fine semolina (see page 221)
vegetable oil, for deep-frying
6 freshly shucked oysters, on the half shell
12 raw prawns, peeled and deveined,
    but with tails left intact
salt flakes, to taste
3 lemons, cut into cheeks
Chilli Mayonnaise (see page 218),
    for serving

BATTER

150 g self-raising flour
200 ml chilled water

This dish must be eaten straight away, while the batter is still hot and crisp, so you need to cook the seafood quickly before the zucchini flowers get cold; if possible, cook them at the same time in two pans. The salt and acid from the lemon juice, the crisp texture and the mouth-feel of the oil are all great appetite stimulants, making fritto misto a popular start to meals in Sardinia. You can add fillets of small fish, such as red mullet or small whiting, if you wish.

To make the batter, sift flour into a bowl and slowly add the water, whisking constantly. Pour through a fine sieve and set aside.

Cut squid hoods open. Using the back of a knife, scrape off the membrane from inside the hoods. Trim off the base, then score the inside of the hoods in a cross-hatch pattern and slice into 3 cm × 2 cm strips; discard tentacles.

Trim the end off each small zucchini. Gently open the flower petals, being careful not to bruise them, and pinch off the stamen from the centre of each flower, then ease the petals back into shape.

Sift flour and semolina together and set aside.

Heat vegetable oil to 160°C (if you don't have a deep-frying thermometer, test the temperature of the oil by dipping the handle of a wooden spoon into it – when bubbles form around the spoon, the oil is hot enough).

Remove oysters from shells, then place oyster shells in a heatproof bowl and cover with boiling water.

Whisk batter briefly, then, holding zucchini flowers by the zucchinis, dip into the batter, and gently wipe up the side of the bowl to remove excess batter. Lower carefully into hot oil and deep-fry for about 4 minutes, until underside is golden, then turn and fry other side for 2–3 minutes, until golden. Drain on paper towel.

Toss prawns, squid and oysters in the flour and semolina mixture. Dust off any excess, then deep-fry in batches, being careful not to overcrowd the pan, for a minute or two until underside is golden. Turn and fry the other side for a further minute or two. Drain on paper towel.

Drain oyster shells, and return an oyster to each shell. Arrange in a serving bowl, along with prawns, squid and zucchini flowers. Sprinkle with salt, and serve immediately with lemon cheeks and chilli mayonnaise on the side.

CLAM AND CHICKPEA SOUP

ZUPPA DI CECI E ARSELLE

SERVES 6 AS A FIRST COURSE

300 g dried chickpeas, soaked in water
  overnight
100 g desiree potato (1 small), peeled
  and halved
⅓ cup (80 ml) extra virgin olive oil,
  plus extra for drizzling
1 kg vongole (clams), purged
  (see page 221)
4 cloves garlic, finely sliced
½ leek, washed well and cut into fine strips
1 small red chilli, finely sliced
4 roma (plum) tomatoes, peeled,
  tops cut off, seeded and chopped
salt flakes, to taste
2 sprigs rosemary, leaves picked
  and very finely chopped
1 tablespoon finely sliced flat-leaf
  parsley leaves
finely grated zest of 1 lemon
crusty bread, for serving

In Sardinia this dish would be made with very small clams called *arselle*, which are harvested from along the water's edge. The closest we get to these are vongole; they're generally a bit larger, so buy the smallest ones you can find. You'll need to start this recipe a day ahead to give the chickpeas time to soak.

Place chickpeas and their soaking water in a saucepan and add potato. Bring to the boil, reduce heat and simmer for 45–60 minutes, until chickpeas are tender, skimming regularly to remove any froth that rises to the surface. Drain, reserving cooking water.

Heat a large frying pan over high heat until very hot, add half the oil, then the vongole, cover, shake pan well and cook for a minute or two, until most of the shells open. Remove from heat. Fish out any vongole that haven't opened and, using a blunt knife such as a butter knife, gently prise them open: if the meat is plump and intact on one side of the shell, use them; otherwise discard them. Remove vongole meat from shells. Strain cooking juices and set aside.

Heat a saucepan over low–medium heat, add remaining oil and, when hot, add garlic, leek and chilli and cook for 5–10 minutes, until leek is soft. Add chickpeas, reserved vongole cooking juices, tomato and 3 cups (750 ml) of the reserved chickpea cooking water. Bring to the boil, then reduce heat and simmer for 15 minutes, skimming regularly to remove any froth that rises to the surface.

Meanwhile, place potato in a food processor with a ladleful of the chickpea mixture from the frying pan. Add just enough of the reserved chickpea cooking water to cover, then pulse until smooth.

Stir the potato mixture into the soup, bring to the boil, then reduce heat and simmer for a further 5 minutes. Stir in vongole meat, salt, rosemary, parsley and lemon zest. Remove from heat and set aside to rest, partially covered, for 5 minutes.

Ladle into soup bowls, drizzle with olive oil and serve with crusty bread on the side.

SARDINIAN SEAFOOD SOUP

SA CASSOLA

1 × 600 g piece blue-eye trevalla fillet, skin off

3 × 100 g squid, cleaned and skinned

100 ml extra virgin olive oil, plus extra for drizzling

½ brown onion, finely chopped

2 cloves garlic, finely sliced

1 small red chilli, finely sliced

1 teaspoon dried Greek oregano (see page 220)

6 baby octopus, cleaned and halved

3 small blue swimmer crabs, cleaned and halved

12 raw prawns, peeled and deveined, but with tails left intact

12 saucer scallops, trimmed

24 vongole (clams), purged (see page 221)

24 blue mussels, scrubbed lightly with a scourer

pane carasau (see page 6), for serving

salt flakes, to taste

1 cup (250 ml) Vermentino (see page 219) or other dry white wine

3 cups (750 ml) Passata (see page 218)

20 basil leaves, torn

Seafood soups that are so hearty they're more like stews are served as main courses all over the Mediterranean. The general Italian name is *zuppa di pesce* (literally 'seafood soup'), but in Sardinia such dishes are called *burrida* in the south, and *cassola* in the north, where I come from. It's very important that you don't stir the soup once the seafood goes in – at the most, give it a shake to make sure everything is cooking evenly – otherwise the seafood will break up and ruin the appearance of the dish.

Preheat oven to 200°C.

Remove any small bones from the fish fillet using a pair of fish tweezers, then trim off and discard the belly flap. Cut into 6 pieces.

Cut squid hoods open. Using the back of a knife, scrape off the membrane from inside the hoods. Trim off the base, score the inside of the hoods in a cross-hatch pattern and cut into 3 cm pieces; halve tentacles.

Heat a large saucepan, add oil and, when hot, add onion, garlic, chilli and oregano and cook over medium heat until onion is soft but not coloured. Add all the seafood to the onion mixture, and cook for 1 minute.

Meanwhile, drizzle pane carasau with oil, sprinkle with salt flakes, wrap in foil and place in oven for about 5 minutes, until warm.

Add wine to pan and cook for a minute or 2 until it starts to boil. Add passata, return to the boil, then reduce heat and cover. Shake pan well and simmer for about 2 minutes, shaking occasionally, until most of the mussels and vongole open and the crab shell turns orange.

Remove from heat. Fish out any mussels and vongole that haven't opened and, using a blunt knife such as a butter knife, gently prise them open: if the meat is plump and intact on one side of the shell, use them; otherwise discard them. Remove meat from half the mussels and vongole shells, pull off the 'beards' from the mussels, then return all the mussels and vongole to the pan.

Scatter basil over the soup and serve with pane carasau.

BLUE MUSSEL AND FREGOLA SOUP

ZUPPETTA DI COZZE CON FREGOLA

SERVES 6 AS A FIRST COURSE

10 female zucchini (courgette) flowers,
   with baby zucchini attached

fine sea salt, for pasta water

300 g fregola (see page 106)

2 tablespoons extra virgin olive oil,
   plus extra for drizzling

1 clove garlic, finely sliced

1 small red chilli, finely sliced

1.5 kg blue mussels, scrubbed lightly
   with a scourer

100 ml Vermentino (see page 219)
   or other dry white wine

200 g grape tomatoes, tops cut off, halved

3 cups (750 ml) Fish Stock (see page 213)

1 tablespoon finely sliced flat-leaf
   parsley leaves

freshly ground black pepper, to taste

If you debeard mussels before they're cooked you often tear the meat. It's easier to cook the mussel and then the beard easily comes away. The best way to do this is to gently hold the shell of the cooked mussel closed with the beard protruding and then pull lightly on the beard to remove it.

Remove baby zucchini from zucchini flowers, trim off the ends then slice thinly. Gently open the flower petals, being careful not to bruise them, and pinch off the stamen from the centre of each flower. Thinly slice the petals and set aside.

Bring a large saucepan of water to the boil, add salt, then fregola and boil for about 5 minutes from the time the water returns to the boil, until almost cooked (it will finish cooking in the soup). Strain well, toss with a little of the oil and set aside.

Heat a large saucepan over low–medium heat, add remaining oil and, when hot, add sliced zucchini, garlic and chilli and cook for a few minutes, until soft but not coloured. Increase heat, stir in mussels and wine and cook for a minute or two until the liquid starts to boil. Cover, shake pan well and cook for a further few minutes, shaking occasionally, until most of the shells open. Remove from heat. Fish out any mussels that haven't opened and, using a blunt knife such as a butter knife, gently prise them open: if the meat is plump and intact on one side of the shell, use them; otherwise discard them. Pull off the 'beards', leaving the mussels in their shells.

Return mussels to pan, stir in tomatoes, fregola and stock and bring to the boil. Remove from heat, then stir in parsley, shredded zucchini flowers and pepper.

Ladle soup into bowls, drizzle with olive oil and serve.

SQUID FILLED WITH FREGOLA, OLIVES AND PINE NUTS

CALAMARI RIPIENI DI FREGOLA, OLIVE E PINOLI

SERVES 4 AS A FIRST COURSE

fine sea salt, for pasta water
125 g fregola (see page 106)
½ cup (125 ml) extra virgin olive oil,
    plus extra for dressing rocket
4 × 150 g squid, cleaned and skinned,
    tentacles chopped
45 g pine nuts, toasted (see page 222)
    and roughly chopped
juice and finely grated zest of 1 lemon
200 g Ligurian olives, pitted and chopped
1 tablespoon finely sliced dill
¼ teaspoon dried chilli flakes
1 egg, lightly beaten
1 teaspoon finely sliced basil leaves
1 teaspoon finely sliced flat-leaf
    parsley leaves
1 teaspoon finely sliced mint leaves
salt flakes and freshly ground black
    pepper, to taste
wild rocket, washed and dried, for serving

Calamari, Italian for squid, is derived from *calamo*, the word for quill – a reference to the thin transparent cartilage found inside the squid's body that resembles the feather quills once used for writing. In the restaurant we use fennel fronds in the stuffing instead of dill, because we generally have them on hand, so feel free to use them instead if you prefer.

Bring a large saucepan of water to the boil, add fine sea salt, then fregola and boil for 7–10 minutes, until al dente. Drain well, stir through 2 tablespoons of the oil and set aside to cool.

Heat a frying pan over high heat, add a little of the oil and, when hot, add squid tentacles and toss for 2 minutes. Set aside to cool then combine with fregola, pine nuts, lemon juice and zest, olives, dill, chilli, egg, basil, parsley, mint, salt and pepper.

Fill squid hoods three-quarters-full with fregola mixture and close with a toothpick.

Preheat oven to 180°C.

Heat an ovenproof frying pan over medium heat, add remaining oil and, when hot, add squid and cook, turning as needed, until lightly coloured on all sides. Transfer to oven and cook for 8 minutes, then remove and cut each squid into 3 or 4 slices.

Toss rocket leaves with olive oil, salt flakes and pepper and divide among four plates. Top each plate with a squid and serve.

ROCKLOBSTER CATALAN-STYLE

ARAGOSTA ALLA CATALANA

SERVES 4

2 x 600–800 g live rocklobsters
1 small red onion, finely sliced
150 ml red wine vinegar
100 ml extra virgin olive oil
juice of 1 lemon, strained
salt flakes, to taste
10 truss cherry tomatoes, tops cut off,
    quartered
1 tablespoon flat-leaf parsley leaves

This dish comes from the city of Alghero on Sardinia's northwestern coast, where the best rocklobsters (also called spiny lobsters) are found. Due to its strategic position in the middle of the Mediterranean, Sardinia has a long history of being occupied by foreign forces. In the 14th century, Catalan invaders took over Alghero, and their influence is still apparent today in the architecture, food and even the dialect spoken there. Once you've cooked and cleaned the rocklobsters, which you can do ahead of time, this is a very simple dish that tastes great. The secret lies in not overcooking the rocklobsters.

Place each rocklobster in a plastic bag with a few air holes in it and place in the freezer for 1 hour.

Meanwhile, fill the largest saucepan you have with water and bring to the boil.

Remove one of the rocklobsters from the freezer and take out of its plastic bag. Immerse it in the rapidly boiling water then cover the pan, so the water returns to the boil as quickly as possible. Cook for 7–8 minutes, depending on size. Lift out of the water with a large slotted spoon or fish slice and set aside to cool. Repeat with remaining rocklobster.

Place onion in the vinegar and leave to marinate for about 15 minutes.

Meanwhile, place each rocklobster on a chopping board on its belly with the tail extended. Insert the point of a large heavy knife where the head and tail meet and split the head in half, then turn the rocklobster around and split the tail in half. Wash the head area under gently running water, being careful not to wet the meat. Devein, remove meat from shell and cut into 2 cm chunks. Pat shell dry.

Whisk oil, lemon juice and salt together to form a dressing. Drain onion well.

When ready to serve, combine rocklobster meat, tomato, onion, parsley and dressing. Arrange meat in the rocklobster shells and serve with lobster crackers and picks, so diners can extract the sweet meat from the legs.

Note
The easiest and most humane way to prepare live crustaceans for cooking is to chill them in the freezer for about 1 hour until they become insensible (but not long enough to freeze them). Once chilled, they should be killed promptly by being split in half or dropped into plenty of rapidly boiling water.

PRAWNS WITH TOMATO, CHILLI AND FREGOLONE

GAMBERI AL POMODORINO LEGGERMENTE PICCANTI E FREGOLONE

SERVES 4 AS A FIRST COURSE

fine sea salt, for pasta water
180 g fregolone
⅓ cup (80 ml) extra virgin olive oil
16 raw prawns, peeled and deveined, but with tails left intact (use heads and shells to make the prawn stock)
1 clove garlic, finely sliced
1 small red chilli, finely sliced
20 grape tomatoes, tops cut off, halved
1 cup (250 ml) Prawn Stock (see page 213)
1 tablespoon finely sliced flat-leaf parsley leaves
salt flakes and freshly ground black pepper, to taste

Fregolone is a slightly larger version of fregola (see below); use fregola or large couscous – sometimes called Israeli, or moghrabi, couscous – if fregolone is unavailable.

Bring a large saucepan of water to the boil, add fine sea salt, then fregolone and boil for 10–12 minutes, until al dente. Drain well, then set aside.

Heat a frying pan over medium heat, add half the oil and, when hot, add prawns and cook for about 2 minutes each side, until lightly coloured. Add garlic and chilli and cook for a further few minutes, until soft but not coloured.

Add tomatoes and fregolone and toss together. Add stock, bring to the boil, then reduce heat and simmer for about 5 minutes, crushing tomatoes with a wooden spoon, until slightly thickened. Stir in parsley, remaining oil, salt flakes and pepper.

Divide prawns among four bowls, spoon over the fregolone and sauce and serve.

Fregola and Fregolone

Fregola (or *fregula*) is a clear reminder of the Arabic influence in Sardinia, being very similar to North African couscous – which is also used in Sardinian cooking, especially in the south. Fregola is slightly larger than couscous, and may have been introduced by Ligurian fishermen who migrated from their colony of Tabarka (in what is now Tunisia) to the Sardinian island of San Pietro in the early 1700s. Although today fregola is one of Sardinia's most widely known foods, it is still more typical of the south, where the Arabic influence is more pronounced.

The name comes from the Latin *fricare*, meaning 'to rub', and it is made in a similar way to couscous, in the bottom of a broad, flat-bottomed wooden or terracotta bowl called a *scivedda*. Hard durum wheat flour (*semolina* in Italian) is sprinkled with a little water and rolled in a circular motion between the palms of the hands to form tiny balls of dough (slightly larger balls of semolina are called fregolone). Here the similarity with couscous ends, as fregola is then slowly oven-dried, giving it a lovely nutty aroma and flavour. Look for artisanally produced fregola, which will be rough-textured with an uneven colour, as some pieces roast more than others, rather than the mass-produced 'fregola' with a smoother, more regular shape – some of these aren't even roasted and so lack fregola's distinctive nuttiness (see page 219 for details of where to buy fregola). Fregola is most commonly cooked in broth to make a substantial soup; it needs to be 'rained' into the broth or cooking water (*a pioggia* in Italian) the same way polenta does, so it doesn't clump together.

Meat
and Poultry

As mountain dwellers, Sardinians have always eaten plenty of meat. Animals are a precious commodity in farming communities, however: sheep and goats provide milk and wool, hens lay eggs, and cattle provide milk or pull ploughs, so they aren't killed lightly. Therefore, pork, mutton and wild game (see page 143) are traditionally the most common meats. Pigs are hardy animals, happy to live on whatever scraps a farmer's family can spare, and so almost every household could afford to keep a pig, which would be killed by the family or the travelling butcher in autumn (see page 131). It's been said that the only part of a pig that isn't eaten is the squeal . . . and the practical Sardinians make sure that nothing goes to waste, salting and curing what can't be eaten fresh and using every scrap and off-cut in sausages or hearty ragùs.

As a country of shepherds, Sardinians also love sheep meat – though it rarely comes from sweet young lambs with a lifetime of milk and wool production ahead of them, but rather from older, more flavoursome sheep. Mutton is still the choice of most Sardinians who grew up with its stronger flavour and now prefer it. Sheep are so fundamental to the Sardinian way of life, that a common expression is *Ogni pastore conosce le sue pecore* ('Every shepherd knows his own sheep'). Goat meat is also popular (see page 112), as these hardy animals will live on household scraps or graze on rocky barren ground, surviving on plants that wouldn't sustain sheep or cattle. Until recently beef was rarely eaten, as Sardinia's rocky landscape isn't suitable for grazing cattle and they were kept mainly as work animals, not for meat.

Spit-roasting, which originated as a simple way for shepherds in the mountains to cook with minimal equipment, is still a popular way of cooking meat. Aromatic woods including olive, oak and myrtle are often used to make the spit, as well as to cook the meat over. Again, nothing is wasted and offal dishes, like *revea* (Spit-roasted Lamb Offal; see page 135), are prepared and sold by butchers, ready to be roasted over the coals. Sardinians love festivals and celebrations – any excuse to bring a large crowd of family, friends and neighbours together to eat, drink and socialise. And you often see whole animals roasting on spits as entire villages come together to celebrate a saint's day, the harvest or a wedding. Such occasions call for something special, and this is when a young animal will be killed and spit-roasted – most often a suckling pig, seasoned simply with some of the island's wild herbs.

But really, any occasion offers a reason to eat and drink, and one of the things I miss most about Sardinia is casual weekend lunches with friends (*spuntino*). These usually involved cooking a sheep or a pig together; add some good wine and a communal sing-along and we'd often sit up until 3 or 4 the next morning, feasting and drinking – and often eating cheese. Mutton and Fregola Soup, Boiled Mutton and Vegetables (see page 120) is commonly eaten at such a gathering: the sheep is boiled and the broth is used to make a soup for the first course (*primo*) by boiling fregola or some small pasta such as ditali or pastina in it, then the meat is eaten with the potato and onion as the main course (*secondo*). Alternatively, the broth can be used to make Gallurese-style Bread Pudding (see page 15). A similar dish, served over two courses so nothing goes to waste, is made with a hen (see page 139).

See also
- Ciciones Pasta with Pork Sausage Sauce (page 23) in 'Pasta and Rice'
- Talluzzas Pasta with Braised Baby Goat (page 37) in 'Pasta and Rice'
- Rice with Pork and White Wine (page 40) in 'Pasta and Rice'
- Veal-stuffed Eggplant (page 51) in 'Vegetables'

KID COOKED 'SHEPHERD-STYLE'

CAPRETTO ALLA MODA DEL PASTORE

1 × 1.2 kg leg baby goat, deboned
1 tablespoon finely sliced mint leaves
2 tablespoons finely chopped
    rosemary leaves
1 tablespoon finely sliced sage leaves
1 tablespoon thyme leaves
1 teaspoon fennel seeds, roughly crushed
1 clove garlic, finely sliced
salt flakes and freshly ground black
    pepper, to taste
plain flour, for dusting
¼ cup (60 ml) extra virgin olive oil
1 carrot, peeled and roughly chopped
1 brown onion, roughly chopped
1 clove garlic, peeled and bruised
1 cup (250 ml) Vermentino (see page 219)
    or other dry white wine
10 g butter

Note

When roasting meat, getting the cooking and resting times right (see page 222) will make a big difference to the end result.

The Italian word for shepherd, *pastore*, comes from the same root as pasture, so a *pastore* may herd any animals that graze the pastures – sheep, goats or even cows – and this dish is commonly cooked with both lamb and kid. It can be served with Chicory with Citrus (see page 65), Braised Fennel (see page 115), Raw Vegetable Salad (see page 61) or, as in the photo, my mum's Potato and Onion Salad (see page 64). You'll need kitchen string for this recipe: use a natural, non-dyed string, as nylon string will melt. Most halal butchers stock goat, and some other butchers will order it on request.

Remove meat from fridge 1–2 hours before cooking. Cover and set aside in a cool place to come to room temperature.

Preheat oven to 180°C.

Lay the meat out, skin-side down, on a clean, dry workbench. Cover with a double layer of plastic wrap and, using a kitchen mallet or rolling pin, beat until 1–2 cm thick. Combine mint, rosemary, sage, thyme, fennel seeds, sliced garlic, salt and pepper and spread over the surface of the meat, patting it in.

Starting from the narrow end, roll up the meat like a swiss roll, tucking the sides in at the widest part to form a neat parcel. Tie with kitchen string to secure. Dust the parcel lightly with flour, shaking off any excess.

Heat a large ovenproof frying pan over high heat, add oil and, when hot, add meat and cook for about 5 minutes, turning to brown on all sides. Remove meat from pan. Add carrot, onion and bruised garlic clove and cook for a minute or two, until starting to colour. Return meat to pan, add wine and bring to the boil, then add ½ cup (125 ml) of water and return to the boil. Cover loosely with foil, transfer to the oven and cook for 30 minutes, then baste and add another ¼ cup (60 ml) of water. Return to the oven and cook for another 30 minutes or so, until a meat thermometer shows 55°C (for medium-rare). Remove meat from oven and increase oven temperature to 200°C.

Remove goat from frying pan (setting aside the pan with the meat juices) and place on a rack set over a baking tray. Cover loosely with foil and leave in a warm place to rest for 20 minutes.

Meanwhile, strain pan juices into a small saucepan, place over medium heat and boil until reduced almost to the consistency of pouring cream. Stir in any juices given off by the resting meat. Whisk in the butter, cover and set aside.

Remove foil and return goat to the oven for 3 minutes. Remove string and cut meat into slices. Arrange on a platter, sprinkle with salt and pour pan juices over the top.

RACK OF LAMB WITH BRAISED FENNEL AND GREEN SAUCE

CARRÈ DI AGNELLO CON FINOCCHI BRASATI E SALSA VERDE

SERVES 4

2 lamb racks
2 tablespoons extra virgin olive oil,
   plus extra for drizzling
salt flakes and freshly ground black
   pepper, to taste

BRAISED FENNEL

2 bulbs baby fennel
2 sprigs thyme
2 cloves garlic, peeled and bruised
salt flakes and freshly ground black
   pepper, to taste
2 cups (500 ml) Vermentino
   (see page 219) or other dry white wine
about 2 cups (500 ml) Vegetable Stock
   (see page 215)

SALSA VERDE

handful basil leaves
small handful mint leaves
handful flat-leaf parsley leaves
25 g salted baby capers, rinsed and dried
3 white anchovy fillets in vinegar, drained
juice of 1 lemon, strained
100 ml extra virgin olive oil
salt flakes and freshly ground black
   pepper, to taste

Note

When roasting meat, getting the
cooking and resting times right (see
page 222) will make a big difference
to the end result.

Carrè refers to the whole rack of lamb, which has seven cutlets. Inevitably, that means there isn't an even number of cutlets – but never mind, there's always someone who wants more and someone who wants less. If you want to portion it equally, though, you can always ask the butcher to cut smaller racks with an even number of cutlets. Ask your butcher to trim the lamb racks of the surface connective tissue, called silverskin, leaving a little of the fat on, and to 'french' the bones but leave them long. Fennel should be served either raw in a salad or meltingly tender, so it's better to overcook it than undercook it here; it should taste almost sticky and caramelised. The fennel doesn't need to be served hot, so it can be cooked in advance and served at room temperature.

For the braised fennel, preheat oven to 160°C. Quarter fennel bulbs, but do not discard the core or the quarters will fall apart. Wash well, place in a small baking dish, together with thyme, garlic, salt and pepper. Add wine and enough stock to just cover – you may not need it all. Press a piece of baking paper onto the surface of the fennel, then cover tightly with a double layer of foil (see page 222). Cook fennel in oven for about 1½ hours, until a wooden skewer can be inserted without any resistance.

Remove meat from fridge 1–2 hours before cooking. Cover and set aside in a cool place to come to room temperature.

When fennel is cooked, remove from oven and loosen the foil slightly, so the steam can escape. Set aside to keep warm. Increase oven temperature to 200°C, ready for the lamb.

Rub the skin-side of the lamb with oil and sprinkle generously with salt, patting it in. Heat an ovenproof frying pan over high heat. Add remaining oil and, when hot, add lamb racks, skin-side down, and cook on each side for about 3 minutes, until well browned. Turn racks over and rest them against each other so the bones interlock. Place pan in oven for about 10 minutes, until a meat thermometer shows 55°C for medium-rare (58°C for medium). Remove from oven (but don't turn oven off), cover pan loosely with foil and set aside to rest for 15 minutes.

Meanwhile, make the salsa verde: pulse all ingredients together in a food processor until a rough paste forms.

Take foil off lamb and return to oven for 4 minutes. Slice lamb racks into individual cutlets and place on a platter with the braised fennel alongside. Drizzle with olive oil, sprinkle with salt and serve with the salsa verde.

LAMB RUMP WITH FREGOLA AND OLIVE SALAD

SELLA DI AGNELLO, INSALATA DI FREGOLA E OLIVE BOSANE

SERVES 4

4 × 300 g lamb rumps, trimmed
    of all except a thin layer of fat
salt flakes and freshly ground black
    pepper, to taste
¼ cup (60 ml) extra virgin olive oil
1 sprig rosemary, leaves picked

FREGOLA AND OLIVE SALAD

fine sea salt, for pasta water
150 g fregola (see page 106)
⅓ cup (80 ml) extra virgin olive oil
1 sprig rosemary, leaves picked
    and finely chopped
1 sprig marjoram, leaves picked
2 sprigs mint, leaves picked and
    finely sliced
1 clove garlic, finely sliced
finely grated zest of 1 orange
20 Bosane olives (see page 219),
    pitted and finely chopped
2 tablespoons aged sweet vinegar
    (see page 220)
salt flakes and freshly ground black
    pepper, to taste

Chefs hate to overcook meat, generally preferring to serve it rare to medium-rare, but rump is a tougher cut that needs to be cooked beyond medium-rare to break down some of the fibres and make it tender; it's ideal cooked to medium. This fregola salad is great served with any roast meat, and is easy to make: just remember to leave the fregola to cool before adding it to the dressing, or the herbs will discolour and ruin the look of the dish.

To cook the fregola for the salad, bring a large saucepan of water to the boil, add fine sea salt, then fregola and boil for about 7–10 minutes, until al dente. Strain well, toss with a little of the oil, then spread out on a tray or large plate and leave until cold.

Remove lamb from fridge 1–2 hours before cooking. Cover and set aside in a cool place to come to room temperature.

Preheat oven to 200°C.

Sprinkle lamb generously with salt all over, patting it in. Heat an ovenproof frying pan over medium–high heat. Add oil and, when hot, add the lamb, skin-side down, and cook on each side for about 2 minutes, until well browned. Place pan in oven for about 15 minutes, until a meat thermometer shows 58°C (for medium). Remove from oven (but don't turn oven off), cover dish loosely with foil and set aside to rest for 20 minutes.

Take foil off lamb and return to oven for 4 minutes.

Meanwhile, combine remaining salad ingredients in a large bowl to make a dressing. Add fregola to bowl and toss well.

Divide fregola among four plates. Remove lamb rumps from frying pan, then cut each one across the grain into 4–5 slices and arrange on top of the fregola. Place frying pan over high heat and bring cooking juices to the boil. Stir in some pepper, then drizzle over the meat. Garnish with a few rosemary leaves.

Note
When roasting meat, getting the cooking and resting times right (see page 222) will make a big difference to the end result.

LAMB SHOULDER WITH RAW VEGETABLE SALAD

SPALLA DI AGNELLO CON INSALATA DI PINZIMONIO

SERVES 4

1 × 1.5–2 kg shoulder baby lamb, trimmed
4 cloves garlic, peeled and quartered
   lengthways
16 small sprigs rosemary, ideally the tops
   of the stems with just 6–10 leaves each
20 slices flat pancetta
2 tablespoons extra virgin olive oil,
   plus extra for drizzling
salt flakes and freshly ground black
   pepper, to taste
Raw Vegetable Salad (see page 61),
   for serving
2 lemons, cut into cheeks

You can ask your butcher to trim the lamb of any excess fat and the surface connective tissue, called silverskin, or do it yourself with a small sharp knife. You don't need to get rid of all the fat. Leave a little on to keep the meat moist and add flavour – it will melt away during the long, slow cooking. The garlic and rosemary studded into the meat imparts a delicious flavour and aroma.

Remove lamb from fridge 1–2 hours before cooking. Cover and set aside in a cool place to come to room temperature.

Preheat oven to 160°C.

Using a thin sharp knife, make 16 evenly spaced incisions in the lamb shoulder, then poke a quarter of a garlic clove and a small sprig of rosemary into each incision.

Lay pancetta slices over the top of the lamb, overlapping them slightly and tucking the ends underneath. Gently rub oil over the pancetta and the underside of the lamb, sprinkle well with salt and pepper and place on a rack in a roasting tin. Pour 2 cups (500 ml) of water into the roasting tin – the rack should be high enough to prevent the water from touching the lamb. Cover tightly with a double layer of foil (see page 222), and cook in oven for about 2 hours, until the meat is coming away from the bone; check after 1½ hours and top up the water if necessary.

Remove lamb from oven and loosen the foil slightly, so the steam can escape; set aside to rest for 15 minutes. Increase oven temperature to 200°C.

Take foil off lamb and return to oven for 5–10 minutes, until pancetta is crisp.

Using a slotted spoon, pile salad onto one side of a platter, discarding any excess dressing, and place lamb shoulder on the other side. Shred lamb meat from the bone, drizzle with olive oil and serve with lemon cheeks on the side.

Note
When roasting meat, getting the cooking and resting times right (see page 222) will make a big difference to the end result.

MUTTON AND FREGOLA SOUP, BOILED MUTTON AND VEGETABLES

PECORA IN CAPPOTTO CON FREGOLA

SERVES 6

1 × 2.5 kg shoulder mutton,
   cut into 14 pieces
salt flakes and freshly ground black
   pepper, to taste
6 roma (plum) tomatoes, tops cut off,
   halved
3 brown onions, peeled and quartered
4 kipfler potatoes, peeled and halved
   lengthways
3 carrots, peeled and cut into 5 cm pieces
3 stalks celery heart, cut into 5 cm pieces
300 g fregola (see page 106)
extra virgin olive oil, for drizzling
2 lemons, cut into cheeks

The name of this dish literally means 'sheep in a coat', as the meat is boiled under a 'coat' of potatoes and onions. Young lamb is never used, it's always the older mutton, which has a stronger flavour and aroma . . . just the way Sardinians like it. This is a typical peasant dish where nothing goes to waste: once the meat is boiled, fregola is added to the cooking liquid to make a soup for the first course, then the mutton is eaten with the vegetables as a second course. You'll need a stockpot or large saucepan for this dish, as there's quite a bit of meat.

Remove mutton from fridge 1 hour before cooking. Cover and set aside in a cool place to come to room temperature.

Wash mutton well in cold water, then place in a large saucepan and cover with cold water. Add 1 tablespoon salt and the tomatoes, then place over high heat and bring to the boil. Reduce heat and simmer for 1½ hours, skimming regularly to remove any froth that rises to the surface and crushing tomatoes occasionally with a wooden spoon.

Add onion and potato and cook for a further 30 minutes. Add carrot and celery and cook for a further 15 minutes or so, until vegetables are tender and meat is falling off the bone. Stir in salt.

Using a slotted spoon, remove meat and vegetables from stock and arrange on a serving platter. Cover with foil, place in oven and turn it to 60°C to keep warm.

Strain stock into a clean saucepan, discarding any solids. Bring to the boil, stir in fregola and cook for about 7–10 minutes, until al dente.

Add salt, ladle into soup bowls, drizzle with olive oil and serve as a first course.

Remove platter of meat and vegetables from oven, sprinkle with salt and pepper, drizzle with olive oil and serve with lemon cheeks as a second course.

FILLET OF BEEF WITH TURNIP TOPS, BOTTARGA BUTTER AND RED WINE SAUCE

FILETTO DI MANZO CON CIME DI RAPA, BURRO ALLA BOTTARGA E SALSA AL CANNONAU

SERVES 4

1 × 800 g piece beef eye fillet, trimmed
⅓ cup (80 ml) extra virgin olive oil
salt flakes and freshly ground black
   pepper, to taste
2 bunches cime di rapa,
   cut into 8 cm lengths
1 clove garlic, peeled and bruised
finely grated zest of 1 lemon
½ cup (125 ml) Cannonau (see page 219)
   or other full-bodied red wine

BOTTARGA BUTTER

20 g bottarga (see page 93),
   freshly grated, sifted
150 g butter, at room temperature

Note

When roasting meat, getting the cooking and resting times right (see page 222) will make a big difference to the end result.

Cime di rapa (also called turnip tops or broccoli rabe) is a dark, leafy green vegetable; if unavailable, use chicory, cavolo nero or spinach. This is an interesting dish because it combines bottarga with meat; ask your butcher to trim the beef fillet of the surface connective tissue called silverskin and most excess fat. This bottarga butter is also great melted over any seafood or tossed through pasta – it keeps well in the freezer and adds a Sardinian flavour to almost anything, including vegetables.

Remove beef from fridge 1–2 hours before cooking. Cover and set aside in a cool place to come to room temperature.

Meanwhile, to make bottarga butter, mix bottarga into butter until well combined. Place a large piece of plastic wrap on a clean, dry workbench. Spoon butter in a long strip along the centre of the plastic and fold one end over to enclose the butter. Holding the sides of the plastic, roll into a neat log about 2.5 cm in diameter, then twist ends firmly to secure and refrigerate until needed.

Preheat oven to 110°C. Rub half the oil all over the beef fillet and sprinkle generously with salt all over, patting it in. Heat an ovenproof frying pan over high heat until very hot, add a little oil, then the beef and cook for about 4 minutes, until well browned. Turn meat over and cook for a few minutes, until well browned, then brown each side for a minute or two. Turn back onto original side, and place in oven for about 45 minutes, until a meat thermometer shows 55°C (medium-rare).

Remove beef from oven and increase oven temperature to 160°C. Place beef on a cooling rack set over the frying pan. Cover loosely with foil and set aside in a warm place to rest for 20 minutes.

Meanwhile, place cime di rapa in boiling, salted water and cook until stems are tender – about 4 minutes from the time the water returns to the boil. Drain well and plunge into iced water to cool. Remove from water, squeeze out well and set aside. Heat a frying pan over medium heat, add remaining oil and, when hot, add garlic and cook for 1 minute. Add cime di rapa and toss well for about 2 minutes to reheat. Add lemon zest, pepper and plenty of salt. Cover and set aside to keep warm.

Slice bottarga butter into 8 discs and set aside.

Uncover meat, place on a baking tray and return to oven for 6 minutes to reheat.

Meanwhile, place frying pan containing meat cooking and resting juices over high heat. Add wine and stir well to remove any bits from the base of the pan, then boil for a minute or two until slightly reduced. Pour into a small sauce jug.

Remove meat from oven, cut into 8 slices and top each slice with a disc of bottarga butter. Serve with cime di rapa and the sauce alongside.

BEEF RIB EYE WITH MUSHROOM SAUCE

COSTATA DI MANZO CON RAGÙ AI FUNGHI MISTI

SERVES 4

4 × 250 g beef rib eye steaks
2 cups (500 ml) Vermentino
  (see page 219) or other dry white wine
300 g mixed mushrooms, trimmed
  and sliced
8 juniper berries
large handful flat-leaf parsley leaves
salt flakes and freshly ground black
  pepper, to taste
2 tablespoons extra virgin olive oil
pinch freshly grated nutmeg
25 g butter

Note

When roasting meat, getting the
cooking and resting times right (see
page 222) will make a big difference
to the end result.

This is a great dish to cook on a barbecue – the meat is best cooked medium-rare. Ask your butcher to trim the beef of any surface connective tissue, called silverskin. Use a combination of mushrooms for this dish, such as oyster, shiitake, swiss brown, enoki and king browns. Enoki mushrooms, which are generally considered to be Asian, also grow in Sardinia, where they are called *chiodini*, which means 'small nails' – exactly what they look like.

Place steaks in a glass or ceramic dish. Combine wine, mushrooms, juniper and parsley and pour over meat. Cover and leave in fridge to marinate for 3 hours, turning meat after 1½ hours.

Remove from fridge and set aside for 1–2 hours to come to room temperature. Remove steaks from marinade and pat dry. Drain the mushrooms and parsley, reserving them and the marinade.

Heat a barbecue grill-plate or char-grill pan until it is very hot. Sprinkle meat well with salt on both sides, patting it in. Cook for 4 minutes each side, then remove to a rack set over a baking tray, cover loosely with foil and set aside to rest for 15 minutes.

Pour any meat juices that collect on the baking tray into the marinade. Heat a frying pan over high heat, add oil and, when hot, add mushrooms and parsley and cook for 5–10 minutes, until mushrooms are well browned and slightly crisp. Add salt and half the reserved marinade and boil until slightly thickened and reduced by about half. Stir in pepper, nutmeg and butter and set aside.

Return steaks to the hot barbecue for 1 minute each side, then serve with mushroom sauce on the side.

OVEN-ROASTED SUCKLING PIG WITH SCENTED APPLE SAUCE

PORCETTO ARROSTO CON SALSA ALLE MELE

Porcetto (pronounced por-chet-o) is a suckling pig, no larger than 10 kg. A classic Sardinian dish, this was on the menu of my first restaurant, Cala Luna, where I only cooked a few traditional dishes. While it's sometimes served with a drizzle of bitter honey, apple sauce isn't a traditional accompaniment, but I served it this way at Cala Luna due to popular demand. At Pilu at Freshwater, where it has become my most popular dish, I serve it with pickled apple slices, orange mustard fruit and Salsa Verde (see page 115). Raw Vegetable Salad (see page 61) also makes a good accompaniment. It's important to cover the skin well with salt to draw out the moisture and make it crisp, as the skin is too fine to score the way you do with a larger pig. Sardinia is a big cork producer, and this dish is traditionally served on slightly concave cork platters and garnished with myrtle leaves, as in the photo here.

SERVES 8

½ suckling pig
extra virgin olive oil, for oiling and drizzling
fine sea salt, to taste
rosemary leaves, for garnishing

SCENTED APPLE SAUCE

50 g butter
6 granny smith apples, peeled,
    cored and sliced
¼ cup (55 g) castor sugar
¼ teaspoon ground cinnamon
¼ teaspoon ground cloves
30 ml Cinzano bianco

Notes

Most butchers are reluctant to sell half a suckling pig (so you may be best off to freeze the other half or share with a friend). You'll need to order a 7–8 kg pig, halved lengthways, with the head and trotters removed.

When roasting meat, getting the cooking and resting times right (see page 222) will make a big difference to the end result.

Remove pig from fridge 1–2 hours before cooking. Cover and set aside in a cool place to come to room temperature.

Preheat oven to 110°C. Place pig, skin-side up, on a rack on a large baking tray. Drizzle with a little oil, rubbing it in, and cover skin generously with salt, rubbing it in thoroughly, then leave for about 15 minutes, until skin becomes moist.

Cook on the middle shelf of the oven for 30 minutes, then increase temperature to 150°C and cook for a further 1 hour 20 minutes. Open oven door and reduce temperature to 120°C, leaving door open for about 5 minutes to help temperature to drop. Close door and cook for a further 40 minutes or so, until the meat comes away from the bone on the back leg.

Meanwhile, make the scented apple sauce: melt butter in a saucepan and add apple. Cover and cook over medium heat for 10 minutes, stirring occasionally. Stir in sugar, cinnamon, cloves and Cinzano and boil for 1 minute. Reduce heat to low, cover and cook, stirring occasionally, for 20–30 minutes, until apple is soft but still chunky. Place in a serving bowl, cover and set aside.

Remove pig from oven and increase temperature to 220°C. Cover pig loosely with foil and set aside for at least 15 minutes. Take off foil and, using a clean, dry cloth, brush off all the salt. Clean the roasting rack and place pig, skin-side up, back on the rack on the baking tray. Return to oven for about 30 minutes, until skin is crisp.

Place pig on a clean chopping board and, using a cleaver or poultry shears, cut into about 25 large chunks. Arrange on a serving platter, garnish with rosemary and serve with scented apple sauce on the side.

POLENTA WITH PORK SAUSAGE SAUCE

POLENTA CON RAGÙ DI SALSICCIA

SERVES 6

2 cups (500 ml) milk
salt flakes, to taste
400 g coarse polenta
80 g aged Pecorino Sardo, freshly grated
1 tablespoon finely sliced flat-leaf
    parsley leaves

PORK SAUSAGE RAGÙ

100 ml extra virgin olive oil
1 carrot, peeled and diced
1 stalk celery heart, diced
1 clove garlic, finely sliced
300 g Italian-style pork sausages,
    skins removed
250 g canned peeled tomatoes, drained
¼ teaspoon saffron threads
salt flakes and freshly ground black
    pepper, to taste

Polenta is more often associated with Piedmont than Sardinia. But the Piemontese ruled Sardinia from 1720 until 1861, when the Kingdom of Italy was formed, and Sardinia's cold mountain winters mean that polenta was readily adopted. I like to use polenta di Storo, a particularly coarse polenta from Storo, a village on the border of Trentino and Lombardy; it's available through some delicatessens. You must start eating this dish as soon as the polenta is ready, so the ragù needs to be prepared first. Families will often eat this dish directly from a large platter placed in the centre of the table; when guests are present, they generally spoon a portion onto their plates, going back for second, third or even fourth helpings until the polenta is finished.

To make the pork sausage ragù, heat a frying pan, add oil and, when hot, add carrot, celery and garlic. Cook over low heat, stirring often, for about 5 minutes, until soft and slightly coloured.

Add sausage meat, spread it out evenly in the pan and cook, without stirring, for 5 minutes. Then, using a wooden spoon to break it up, turn the meat over and cook the other side for a few minutes, until browned all over.

Crush tomatoes in your hand over the frying pan and stir them into the sauce, along with the saffron, salt and pepper. Cook for 20 minutes, stirring occasionally, then set aside to keep warm.

Combine milk, salt and 1 litre of water in a large saucepan and bring to the boil. Reduce heat to low, slowly 'rain' in the polenta, whisking constantly. Once all of the polenta is added, cook for 40 minutes, stirring with a wooden spoon every few minutes.

Spread the polenta onto a large wooden board or ceramic platter. Pour the sauce over the top and spread it out to the edges. Scatter pecorino and parsley over the top and serve in the centre of the table for guests to help themselves.

KILLING THE PIG

Many families in Sardinia still keep a pig, feeding it up all year on household scraps and killing it in autumn, usually around November, then preserving the meat to feed the family through the winter, which is traditionally a leaner time. Killing the pig is a weekend-long event involving the whole family. As a child I remember being at my grandfather's house with my parents, siblings, aunts, uncles and cousins for the *faghimus su polcu* ('making the pig').

The pig would be killed by the travelling butcher on Friday and the first thing that needed to be eaten was the blood, so savoury and sweet black puddings were made. When you bled the pig, someone had to whisk the blood so it didn't coagulate, then you made black pudding for Friday night's dinner, mixing the blood with bits of fat pancetta and putting the mixture into the large intestine to make sausages, which were boiled and served with salad and potatoes that night. The rest of the blood was mixed with sultanas, nuts, citrus zest, and sometimes chocolate, to make *sangue dolce* (literally 'sweet blood'), which was served for dessert at the final meal on Sunday. I loved *sangue dolce* when I was a kid, but now I don't have the chance to eat it so often.

The pig would then be split in half and the intestines and tripe stripped out, before it was taken down to the creek and washed in running water. I remember my aunts washing the liver and other offal, being very careful not to break the gall bladder, because if the bitter bile got onto the meat you had to throw it all away. They'd make a dish called *frattaglie alla barbaricina* from mixed offal, heart, kidneys, lungs, all finely chopped and braised in red wine with onions, cloves and other spices.

On Saturday we'd all work really hard breaking the pig down, taking out the ribs, carving the legs and salting them for prosciutto, taking out the belly and seasoning it for pancetta, and chopping the leftover bits of meat for sausages because they had to be marinated with salt and pepper overnight.

On Sunday we'd finish off making the sausages, then we'd make a rice dish with the *pulpedda* (see page 40), the little bits of pork meat leftover from making the sausages, sometimes marinated in red wine. Then the whole family would sit down together to a big dinner with lots of wine – in fact there'd be lots of wine at every dinner over the weekend.

SARDINIAN-STYLE TRIPE

TRIPPA ALLA SARDA

SERVES 6

1 kg honeycomb tripe
2 tablespoons fine sea salt
⅓ cup (80 ml) extra virgin olive oil
2 brown onions, finely sliced
2 cloves garlic, finely sliced
¾ teaspoon dried chilli flakes
400 g canned peeled tomatoes, squashed
2 sprigs mint, leaves picked
80 g aged Pecorino Sardo, freshly grated,
 plus extra for serving
salt flakes, to taste
crusty bread, for serving

Offal is an important part of the Sardinian diet, because nothing is ever wasted, and tripe is particularly popular. I remember going to a trattoria in Oschiri, a town in the centre of northern Sardinia, that sells only tripe, nothing else. Their *Trippa alla Sarda* (literally 'Sardinian tripe') has a red tomato base with lots of pecorino on top, and there are many variations depending on what's in season; they make it with artichokes, broad beans, peas, potatoes . . . but it's always a little bit spicy, from tiny dried chillies. I like to serve tripe with Fried Artichokes (see page 47) on top so the crunch balances the soft, gelatinous nature of the tripe. Tripe is traditionally cooked in a terracotta dish, but not all terracotta can be used on the stovetop, so ask before you buy or at least serve in a terracotta dish.

Trim off the thick ends of the tripe pouches and split each pouch in half.

Bring 6 litres of water to the boil in a large saucepan, add fine sea salt, then tripe. Cover and return to the boil, then reduce heat and simmer, turning occasionally, for about 1 hour, until a wooden skewer can be inserted without any resistance. Drain tripe and, when cool enough to handle, cut into strips about 5 cm long × 1 cm wide.

Heat a large frying pan over low heat, add oil and, when hot, add onion, garlic and chilli and cook until onion is soft and slightly coloured, about 10 minutes. Stir in tripe, increase heat to high and cook for 5 minutes. Stir in 2 cups (500 ml) of water, the tomatoes with their juice, mint leaves and salt. Bring to the boil, then reduce heat to low–medium and simmer for 50–60 minutes, stirring occasionally, until tripe is very tender. Add more water, a little at a time, as it starts to dry out, but only enough to prevent it sticking to the pan; the finished dish should be glossy with a small amount of thick sauce in the bottom of the pan.

Add salt flakes, remembering that the pecorino will be quite salty, then cover and set aside to rest for 20 minutes. Scatter pecorino over the top and serve with crusty bread and extra pecorino on the side.

Note

Tripe is the stomach of various animals. There are three types: smooth or flat (from the first stomach, or rumen); honeycomb (from the second stomach, or reticulum), which is the most common, as it is the tenderest and meatiest; and bible tripe, which has many thin folds or 'leaves' on the surface (from the third stomach, or omasum). Most recipes use either beef or veal tripe, but lamb, goat or pork tripe can also be used. Traditional recipes always say to first wash the tripe because it was usually 'green' (raw), however these days butchers sell tripe already cooked and bleached (also called scalded) and ready for use in recipes such as this.

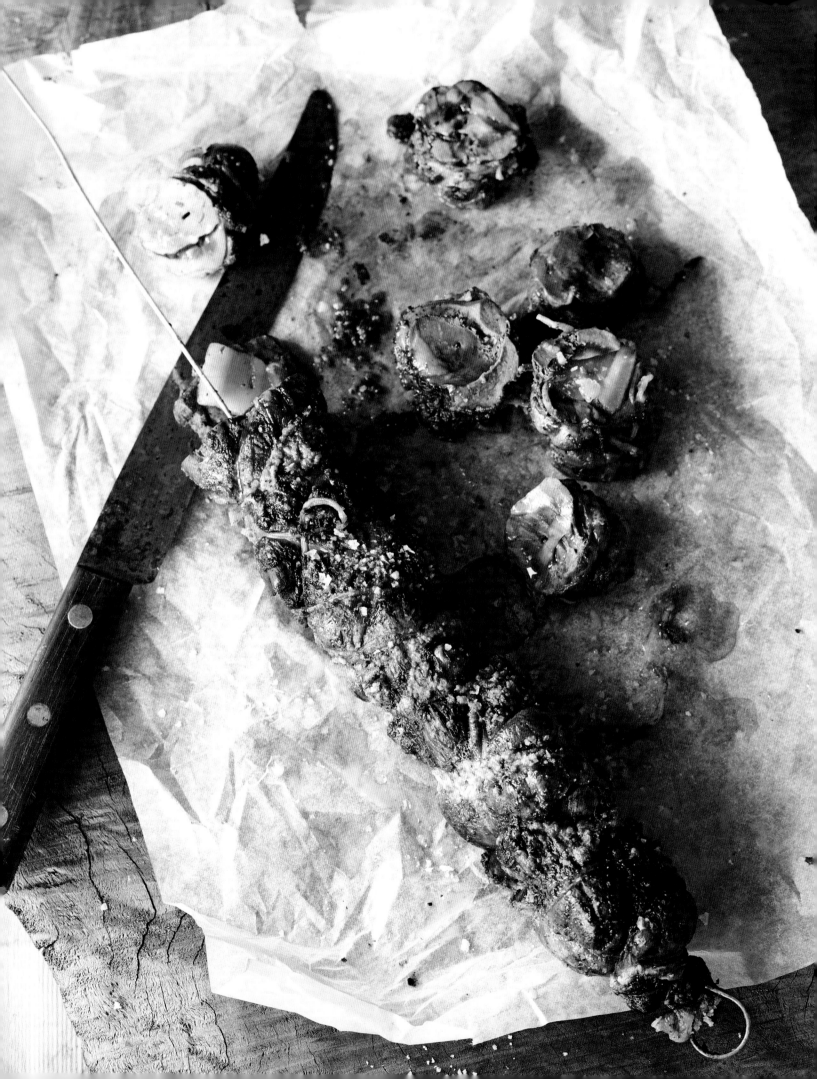

SPIT-ROASTED LAMB OFFAL

REVEA DI AGNELLO

SERVES 6–8 AS PART OF AN ANTIPASTO

4 lamb's kidneys, trimmed of excess fat
150 g lamb's liver
1 lamb's lung, large tube trimmed off
1 lamb's heart, trimmed of excess fat
150 g lardo (see page 220)
100 g caul fat, soaked in warm water
    for a few minutes
2 lamb's intestines
salt flakes, to taste
extra virgin olive oil, for drizzling
crusty bread, for serving

Note

Traditionally this dish was made with
all the innards after a spring lamb was
slaughtered, so the first thing you
needed to do was clean all the offal.
Today, butchers will do this for you
if you ask; you may need to pre-order
the offal from your butcher.

I remember walking into the old stable at my grandfather's place, where this
dish would be cooking over an open fire. It's made all over Sardinia with offal
from very young (suckling) animals: pigs, lambs or goats. It's most common
around Easter, as that's when the baby lambs and goats are around, though it's
also prepared at other times – usually with a suckling pig, as they're available all
year. Either way, it's always for a special gathering; you don't kill a young animal
just for an everyday meal. In some places bread is placed between the pieces of
offal, in other places potatoes are used, but my family's version adds only lardo
to keep it moist. Mostly I remember *revea* being cut into nice little discs and
served on a platter with prosciutto, salami, and *pane carasau* as an antipasto,
though I have also seen it served with the meat from the spit-roasted animal.
You'll need a long, flat metal skewer, so the offal doesn't roll around it, ideally
about 50 cm long by 1 cm wide (they're available from barbecue and hardware
stores). Although *revea* is traditionally cooked on a spit over hot coals, you can
cook it in the oven – or use a barbecue rotisserie, if you have one.

Cut kidneys, liver, lung and heart into pieces roughly 3–4 cm square and about 1 cm
thick. Cut lardo into slices 3–4 cm square and about 5 mm thick.

Thread a slice of lardo onto a long, flat metal skewer, then add pieces of the various
offal, inserting a slice of lardo after every 4–5 pieces. Continue threading the skewer
until all of the offal and lardo has been used.

Preheat oven to 150°C.

Drain the caul fat, pat it dry with paper towel and spread it out on a clean, dry
workbench, overlapping the pieces slightly. Place the skewered offal at one end and
roll the caul fat around it, tucking the ends in to enclose it and trimming if necessary.
Hold the skewer upright and poke the tip of it through one end of the intestine.
Spiral the intestine up, then back down the skewer like string, repeating until both
intestines are used. Tuck the ends under another piece of intestine to secure them.

Place the skewer on a rack over a shallow baking dish and cook on the middle shelf
of the oven for 35 minutes, then turn the skewer and cook for about another
20 minutes, until crisp and golden brown.

Remove from oven, cover loosely with foil and set aside to come to room
temperature. Slide offal off skewer and slice into 2 cm thick discs. Sprinkle
generously with salt, drizzle with olive oil and serve with crusty bread.

HEN AND PEA TERRINE

TERRINA DI GALLINA E PISELLI

SERVES 12 AS A FIRST COURSE

1 × 1.6 kg pullet (young hen)
1 small brown onion, roughly chopped
1 carrot, peeled and roughly chopped
1 stalk celery heart, roughly chopped
3 cloves garlic, sliced
2 litres Chicken Stock (see page 214)
½ bunch flat-leaf parsley
1 small bunch thyme
1 small bunch dill
100 ml red mirto (see page 153)
8 leaves titanium-strength gelatine
150 g chestnuts
500 g rock salt
375 g green peas in pods, shelled
salt flakes and freshly ground black
    pepper, to taste
pane carasau (see page 6), for serving
extra virgin olive oil, for drizzling
pickled vegetables, such as cornichons
    and onions, for serving

Note

Different brands and grades of gelatine leaves have different setting strengths. The amounts given in this recipe are for Gelita brand titanium-strength leaves, which are the most commonly seen; they're available from some delicatessens and speciality food stores.

This dish is always made with a hen, never a rooster, so buy a good free-range or corn-fed pullet (a hen less than a year old) that has plenty of flavour. In Sardinia the hen is wrapped in myrtle leaves to marinate. I haven't seen myrtle for sale, but it grows quite well; if you have some in your garden, place the hen on a bed of leaves in the dish and cover with more leaves once you've poured the mirto over it. Wild fennel would usually be used in the marinade, but dill is a good substitute. You need to start this recipe 2 days before you want to serve it, so the hen can marinate and the terrine has time to set. At the restaurant we pickle fennel to serve with this dish, along with cornichons and pickled onions; mustard fruits also work well. The recipe makes a lot, but it's great for a crowd as you can prepare it ahead of time, and leftovers keep well in the fridge for 3–4 days.

Remove pullet from fridge 20 minutes before cooking. Cover and set aside in a cool place to come to room temperature.

Place onion, carrot, celery, garlic and stock in a stockpot or large saucepan, add most of the parsley, thyme and dill, reserving a little of each of the herbs for later. Add pullet, bring to the boil, then reduce heat and simmer for about 45 minutes until the meat begins to fall off the bones, skimming regularly to remove any froth that rises to the surface. Remove pullet from the stock and place in a glass or ceramic dish. Pour over mirto, then cover and refrigerate overnight.

Strain stock, discarding the solids. Return stock to a clean saucepan and boil until reduced by half. Cool and refrigerate overnight.

Next day, warm stock over low heat. Soak gelatine in a little cold water for about 5 minutes. Squeeze gelatine gently to remove excess water, then add to stock and heat, stirring until gelatine has dissolved. Set aside to cool.

Preheat oven to 200°C. Cut a slit in chestnut shells. Heat an ovenproof frying pan over high heat, add chestnuts and rock salt and toss for a minute. Place in oven and roast for 20–30 minutes until shells start to split, tossing occasionally. Remove from oven, discard salt and wipe out pan. Wrap chestnuts in a clean tea towel and set aside until cool enough to handle, then peel off the shells and brown husks. Return peeled chestnuts to pan and roast in oven for about 10 minutes, stirring occasionally, until golden brown. Cut into thin slices and set aside.

Meanwhile, pick leaves from reserved parsley, thyme and dill; finely slice the parsley and finely chop the dill. Blanch peas in boiling salted water for 2 minutes, then refresh in iced water and drain well. Remove pullet from marinade and coarsely shred meat, discarding skin and bones. Place meat in a bowl with peas, chestnuts, salt, pepper, parsley, thyme and dill. Stir to combine well, adding enough stock to moisten well but not cover the ingredients.

Line a 2-litre terrine mould or loaf tin with plastic wrap, leaving some overhanging all around. Pour the pullet mixture into it and tap the mould gently on the bench to remove any air bubbles. Fold the overhanging plastic wrap over the top and refrigerate for at least 12 hours, preferably overnight.

When ready to serve, preheat oven to 200°C. Drizzle pane carasau with olive oil, sprinkle with salt flakes, wrap in foil and place in oven for about 5 minutes, until warm.

Unfold the plastic wrap from the top of the terrine and invert the mould onto a clean chopping board. Remove plastic wrap and, using a sharp serrated knife, carefully cut the terrine into 2 cm thick slices. Serve with pane carasau and pickled vegetables.

HEN BROTH WITH FREGOLA, POACHED HEN

GALLINA IN BRODO CON FREGOLA

SERVES 4

1 × 1.6 kg pullet (young hen)
1 brown onion, peeled and quartered
1 carrot, peeled and cut
   into 4 cm long strips
1 stalk celery heart,
   cut into 4 cm long strips
1 small bunch flat-leaf parsley,
   leaves picked
4 sun-dried tomatoes
extra virgin olive oil, for drizzling
salt flakes, to taste
4 sprigs mint, leaves picked
150 g fregola (see page 106)

Hens aren't killed every day because they are valued food producers, laying eggs; but they're always on hand in the backyard, and so are killed for festive occasions such as birthdays, first communions, or a visit from a relative or good friend. Still, to kill a *gallina* is a pretty special thing, so you don't waste the delicious broth it was cooked in, but rather turn it into a soup with some fregola and mint. The hen, which would traditionally have been wrapped in mirto branches to rest, is then eaten warm or at room temperature. You'll need muslin and kitchen string for this recipe: use a natural, non-dyed string, as nylon string will melt. Warm Potato and Onion Salad (see page 64) makes a great accompaniment.

Remove pullet from fridge 20 minutes before cooking. Cover and set aside in a cool place to come to room temperature.

Place onion, carrot, celery and parsley in a square of muslin, tie into a small pouch with kitchen string and place in 5 litres of water in a stockpot or large saucepan.

Cross the pullet's legs over at the end of the drumsticks and tie with kitchen string. Place in the water and add sun-dried tomatoes. Bring to the boil, then reduce heat and simmer for about 2 hours until the skin starts to peel from the end of the drumsticks, skimming regularly to remove any froth that rises to the surface. Careully remove pullet from pan and place on a wire rack, loosely covered with foil, to cool slightly.

Meanwhile, strain cooking liquid and measure it. Place in a saucepan and, if there is more than 2 litres, boil until reduced to 2 litres. Set aside.

When pullet is cool enough to handle, break off drumsticks, thighs and wings and arrange on a platter. Cut remaining meat into neat slices and add to the platter. Drizzle with olive oil and sprinkle with salt flakes and half the mint leaves.

Return cooking liquid to the boil, then slowly pour in fregola, stirring constantly. Return to the boil and cook for 7–10 minutes, until al dente. Stir through remaining mint leaves and salt. Ladle into soup bowls and drizzle with olive oil.

Serve the soup while it is hot, then serve the pullet, warm or at room temperature, as a second course.

REGIONE SELVAGGIARE

Hunting and Foraging

As a poor people, Sardinians were always happy to harvest whatever they could from their surroundings. Chestnuts, berries, honey and wild herbs are all still popular ingredients in the cuisine, as is wild game such as boar, rabbit, hare and even small birds. In autumn, after the first rains, families take to the hills with their baskets in search of wild mushrooms, especially the prized porcini. And those living on the coast have always gathered clams, mussels and tiny crabs from along the shoreline for soups and pasta sauces.

Greens, including fennel, chicory, nettles and asparagus, grow wild all over the island. I remember after school, my brother Martino and I would climb over the stone wall behind our house and wander along the pathway collecting handfuls of wild asparagus; afterwards we'd make a frittata with it and have it on *panini* as a snack. All of the classic Sardinian herbs also grow wild: rosemary, bay leaves, juniper berries, mint and sage. One of the most distinctive Sardinian flavours is myrtle, which grows wild everywhere – most people have at least one myrtle tree in their garden. Sardinian myrtle, *Myrtus comminis* (also called common, or true, myrtle) is an evergreen shrub; it's not the same as crepe myrtle or lemon myrtle. The leaves and small branches are often used to wrap roasted meat while it rests to impart a wonderful flavour and aroma, and a few leaves are often added to stocks and soups, in the same way many cuisines use bay leaves.

Game birds, including duck, quail, pigeon, thrush, blackbird and partridge, are popular in Sardinian cooking. When I was a kid my friends and I would bring down small birds with our sling shots. We'd also often stay out late on summer nights catching trout and eels in the creeks – something I don't imagine my son, Martino, or other kids his age would have a clue how to do today!

Hunting season starts in mid-August for small birds such as thrush, pigeon and blackbirds, then there are four Sundays starting from 20 September for quails and partridges. Boar season runs from 1 November to 31 January, but hunting is only allowed on Sundays; it's tightly regulated now as people were coming from all over Europe to hunt boar and the numbers were being decimated. Game, like boar and hare, is often marinated in wine and slowly braised to make it more tender.

See also
- Chicory with Citrus (page 65) in 'Vegetables'
- Baked Mushrooms with Bread and Cured Pork Cheek (page 66) in 'Vegetables'
- Clam and Chickpea Soup (page 97) in 'Seafood'
- Blue Mussel and Fregola Soup (page 100) in 'Seafood'

QUAIL STUFFED WITH CHICKEN LIVERS, FENNEL AND TARRAGON

QUAGLIE RIPIENE DI FEGATINI, FINOCCHIO E DRAGONCELLO

SERVES 4 AS A FIRST COURSE

4 × 300 g quail, tunnel-boned
extra virgin olive oil, for shallow-frying
    and oiling
300 g desiree potatoes, peeled
    and finely diced
1 brown onion, finely diced
1 clove garlic, finely sliced
1 bulb baby fennel, washed well
    and finely diced
200 g chicken livers, cleaned
1 tablespoon finely sliced French tarragon
1 tablespoon finely sliced flat-leaf
    parsley leaves
½ teaspoon dried chilli flakes
finely grated zest of 1 lemon
1 egg, lightly beaten
salt flakes and freshly ground black
    pepper, to taste
8 thin slices flat pancetta
2 tablespoons honey, warmed
4 figs, halved
½ punnet baby tarragon, snipped

Notes

To clean chicken livers, trim off the membrane that joins the two lobes together, along with any greenish or discoloured parts.

French tarragon is usually available from October to April. Make sure you don't buy the tasteless Russian tarragon; if French is unavailable, use dried.

Hunting is a way of life in Sardinia. From the age of ten or twelve my brother Martino and I would go out with a sling shot hunting for small birds with our friends, then we'd build a fire in the forest and cook them up. In those days, sucking the meat off the bones was the best part, but for easier eating, I now like to serve these quail partly deboned (tunnel-boned); your poultry supplier can do this for you.

Remove quail from fridge 20 minutes before cooking. Cover and set aside in a cool place to come to room temperature.

Preheat oven to 220°C.

Heat a frying pan, add oil and, when hot, add potato and cook over medium heat for 5–6 minutes, until brown on all sides. Remove from oil using a slotted spoon and set aside on paper towel to drain.

In the same pan, cook onion, garlic and fennel for about 5 minutes, until soft and lightly coloured. Remove from pan with slotted spoon and place in a bowl, then add potatoes to bowl. Add chicken livers to the same pan and cook for about 2 minutes each side, until lightly coloured. Remove from heat, chop roughly and add to bowl, along with tarragon, parsley, chilli, lemon zest, egg and salt and pepper. Mix to form a moist stuffing that can be moulded into shape. Set aside to cool.

Fill the cavity of each quail with the cooled stuffing. Cross quail legs and secure with a toothpick to keep stuffing in place. Place 2 slices of pancetta on a clean, dry workbench in a cross shape. Place a quail on top, breast-side down, and wrap pancetta around it. Repeat with remaining quail and pancetta. Brush quail with some of the honey and place on an oiled baking tray, breast-side up.

Cook quail in oven for 12 minutes, then brush figs with remaining honey and add to baking tray. Return to oven for another 6 minutes or so, until quail are golden brown and figs are caramelised.

Test to check the quail are fully cooked by piercing a thigh with a skewer – if the juices run clear, the quail are ready.

Arrange 1 quail and 2 fig halves on each plate, drizzle with cooking juices and scatter with baby tarragon.

BOILED PARTRIDGE

PERNICE LESSA

SERVES 4

4 × 350–450 g partridges
8 baby carrots (heirloom varieties,
    if possible)
8 golden baby beetroots
8 small salad onions
8 bay leaves
15 black peppercorns
8 cloves garlic, skin on, bruised
16 pieces (about 60 g) sun-dried tomato
1 small bunch flat-leaf parsley, torn
1 small bunch thyme
200 ml white wine vinegar
100 ml extra virgin olive oil, plus extra
    for drizzling
salt flakes and freshly ground black
    pepper, to taste

When my parents built their house, my father cut down a small juniper tree and peeled the bark off it – just like peeling the stem of an artichoke – so he was left with a beautiful pale wood stand with the branches on it, like a hat rack. When he shot partridges, we'd pluck and gut them then hang them on this stand, head on (because some people eat the head), for at least 24 hours; partridge season is September to October, so it's autumn and cool enough for them to hang in the house. It's important to bleed game birds properly, otherwise they taste too strong. When we went hunting, we had *appendicaccia* (strips of leather with a ring at the end) on our belts; when we killed a game bird we'd hook the ring around their neck and hang them from our belt so they bled as we walked along. Partridges are available from specialty poultry suppliers. Heirloom baby carrots add some welcome colour to this dish – they're available from farmers' markets and some greengrocers – as does a side dish of Chicory with Citrus (shown in the photo here; see page 65).

Remove partridges from fridge 1 hour before cooking. Cover and set aside in a cool place to come to room temperature. Trim and peel carrots and beetroots, leaving a little of the stem attached. Trim and peel salad onions, leaving stems attached.

Rinse the cavities of the partridges well, removing any offal, then wipe out with paper towel to remove as much blood as possible. Trim off the necks.

Bring a large saucepan of water to the boil, add bay leaves, peppercorns, garlic, sun-dried tomato, parsley, thyme, carrots, beetroots and spring onions, and return to the boil. Add partridges, return to the boil, then reduce heat and simmer for 15–20 minutes, until the meat peels away from the end of the drumsticks, skimming regularly to remove any froth that rises to the surface.

Remove from heat. Using a slotted spoon, lift partridges out of water and place in a colander to drain for 5 minutes. Drain vegetables in a separate colander, discarding garlic, parsley, thyme and sun-dried tomato. Transfer vegetables to a bowl, cover and refrigerate until required.

Place partridges in a glass or ceramic bowl, add vinegar and olive oil, pouring some into the cavities, and season with salt and pepper. Cover and refrigerate for 1 hour, then turn in the dressing, basting well, and refrigerate for a further hour. Remove from dressing and refrigerate until needed.

Remove partridges and vegetables from fridge 30 minutes before serving. Divide vegetables among four plates, then place a partridge on each plate. Drizzle with olive oil, sprinkle with salt and pepper and serve.

ROAST DUCK WITH CHESTNUTS

ANATRA ARROSTO CON CASTAGNE

SERVES 2

1 × 1.8 kg duck
salt flakes and freshly ground black
    pepper, to taste
1 sprig rosemary
2 sprigs oregano
5 bay leaves
3 sprigs thyme
3 cloves garlic, bruised
⅓ cup (80 ml) extra virgin olive oil

CHESTNUT PURÉE

250 g chestnuts
1 teaspoon extra virgin olive oil
2 teaspoons butter
½ golden shallot, finely diced
1 small clove garlic, finely sliced
1 small desiree potato, peeled
    and roughly chopped
3 sprigs thyme, leaves picked
1 cup (250 ml) Chicken Stock
    (see page 214)
50 ml pouring cream
salt flakes and freshly ground black
    pepper, to taste

SAUCE

2 tablespoons extra virgin olive oil
1 carrot, peeled and roughly chopped
1 stalk celery, roughly chopped
1 brown onion, roughly chopped
⅓ cup (80 ml) red mirto (see page 153)
600 ml Chicken Stock (see page 214)

Note

When roasting meat, getting the
cooking and resting times right (see
page 222) will make a big difference
to the end result.

In Sardinia ducks are always wild, never farmed, or at least they're not farmed for meat – the only ducks we ever kept in the yard were used for eggs. You can prepare the duck and sauce for this dish a day ahead and then assemble it just before serving; if you do this, remove the duck from the fridge 30–60 minutes before reheating to bring it to room temperature. The chestnut purée recipe makes more than you'll need, but the leftovers are great as a dip with bread, crackers or raw vegetables.

Preheat oven to 160°C. Rinse cavity of duck and remove any excess fat from the opening. Season cavity well with salt and pepper, then place rosemary, oregano, bay leaves, thyme and garlic inside. Rub duck skin all over with some of the oil and sprinkle generously with salt and pepper, rubbing it in well. Place on a rack in a roasting tin. Cover tightly with a double layer of foil (see page 222) and roast in oven for 1 hour and 45 minutes before checking to see if duck is cooked. The meat should be coming away from the end of the drumstick; if it isn't, cover again and return to oven for a further 10–15 minutes then check again. Remove from oven and loosen the foil slightly, so the steam can escape. Set aside to rest for 30 minutes.

Meanwhile, make the chestnut purée. Cut a slit in the chestnut shells, then place chestnuts in a saucepan of water and boil for about 20 minutes until shells loosen. Using tongs, remove a chestnut from the water and peel off the shell and brown husk. Set aside, then repeat with remaining chestnuts (leaving the chestnuts in the water makes them easier to peel). Heat oil and butter in a frying pan over medium heat. When hot, add shallot and garlic, reduce heat to low and cook for about 5 minutes, until soft but not coloured. Add potato, thyme and most of the chestnuts, reserving a couple for garnish. Cook for 5 minutes, stirring occasionally, then add three-quarters of the stock. Bring to the boil, reduce heat and simmer for about 45 minutes, until chestnuts are soft. Place in a blender with cream, salt and pepper and process to a smooth purée. Pass through a fine sieve. The chestnut purée should be the texture of pouring cream; if it's too thick, add a little of the remaining stock.

Lay duck on a chopping board, breast-side up. Using a sharp knife, make an incision along the centre of the breast all the way through to the bone then, using the knife and your fingers, ease the breast meat away from the rib cage; the wing and leg will come away with the breast. Repeat on the other side so that the duck is now in 3 pieces: 2 pieces, each with a wing and drumstick attached, plus the carcass. Reserve the carcass and herbs for the sauce, then cut the 2 pieces of duck in half to give 2 wing portions and 2 drumstick portions. Set aside.

To make the sauce, heat a large frying pan over high heat, add oil and, when hot, add carrot, celery and onion. Reduce heat to medium and cook for 10 minutes or so, until well coloured. Break duck carcass into large pieces and add to the pan, along with the herbs from the duck's cavity. Cook for a further 5 minutes, stirring occasionally. Add mirto and stir well to remove any bits stuck to the base of the pan. Bring to the boil and cook for a few minutes before adding the stock. Bring to the boil, then reduce heat and simmer for 30 minutes. Strain through a fine sieve into a saucepan, discarding solids but reserving bay leaves for garnish. Return to the boil, then simmer for 30 minutes, skiming off the fat that rises to the surface.

Clean the frying pan then place over high heat, add remaining oil and, when hot, add the 4 pieces of duck, skin-side down. Reduce heat to low–medium and cook for 3–4 minutes until skin is crisp and duck is heated through.

Slice each wing portion of duck into 3 pieces. Divide sauce between plates, top each with a wing and a drumstick portion of duck, then garnish with reserved chestnuts and bay leaves. Serve with chestnut purée on the side.

STRACCI PASTA WITH BRAISED RABBIT SAUCE AND CHESTNUTS

STRACCI DI PASTA CON RAGÙ DI CONIGLIO E CASTAGNE

SERVES 4 AS A FIRST COURSE

6 chestnuts
500 g rock salt
½ quantity Fresh Pasta Dough #1
   (see page 217), passed through pasta
   machine four times
tipo 00 flour, for dusting
25 g butter
fine sea salt, for pasta water
100 g aged Pecorino Sardo, freshly grated
extra virgin olive oil, for drizzling

BRAISED RABBIT SAUCE

1 × 800 g rabbit, skinned, gutted
   and head removed
plain flour, for dusting
¼ cup (60 ml) extra virgin olive oil
3 golden shallots, roughly chopped
3 cloves garlic, roughly sliced
1 stalk celery heart, roughly chopped
⅓ cup (80 ml) Vermentino (see page 219)
   or other dry white wine
2 cups (500 ml) Chicken Stock
   (see page 214)
¼ bunch thyme, leaves picked
4 canned peeled tomatoes, squashed
salt flakes and freshly ground black
   pepper, to taste

Be careful when cutting rabbit, as the bones are fragile and can splinter, resulting in shards of bone in the sauce: use a sharp kitchen knife and cut by resting the blade on the bone and tapping the back of the knife with a kitchen mallet, or ask your butcher to section the rabbit for you. Chestnuts are traditionally foraged for in winter; in spring, I use new baby broad beans or peas instead. You really need a mouli to make this sauce properly. Stracci literally means 'rags', as this pasta is cut into uneven shapes like torn bits of rag; hand-rolled macaroni (see page 32) is also good with this sauce.

Remove rabbit from fridge 1 hour before cooking. Cover and set aside in a cool place to come to room temperature.

Preheat oven to 200°C. Cut a slit in chestnut shells. Heat an ovenproof frying pan over high heat, add chestnuts and rock salt and toss for a minute. Place in oven and roast for 20–30 minutes until shells start to split, tossing occasionally. Remove from oven, discard salt and wipe out pan. Wrap chestnuts in a clean tea towel and set aside until cool enough to handle, then peel off the shells and brown husks. Return peeled chestnuts to pan and roast in oven for about 10 minutes, stirring occasionally, until golden brown. Cut into thin slices and set aside. Reduce oven to 160°C.

To make the braised rabbit sauce, section the rabbit by removing the legs and thighs then cutting the remaining body into quarters. Dust rabbit pieces lightly with flour, shaking off any excess. Heat a frying pan over medium heat, add oil and, when hot, add rabbit and cook for a few minutes on each side until golden brown. Remove from pan, place in a baking dish and set aside. Add shallot, garlic and celery to the pan and cook for 8–10 minutes, until lightly coloured. Add wine and stir well to remove any bits stuck to the base of the pan. Bring to the boil, then add stock, thyme, tomatoes, salt and pepper and return to the boil. Pour sauce over rabbit, cover baking dish tightly with a double layer of foil (see page 222) and cook in oven for about 1 hour, until the meat is falling off the bone.

Meanwhile, lay a sheet of pasta dough on a clean, dry workbench. Using a wheel pastry cutter, cut the dough into uneven pieces; bite-sized is good, but stracci can be any size. Dust lightly with flour and set aside.

Remove rabbit from sauce and set aside. Pass sauce through a mouli into a clean saucepan – it should be the consistency of thickened cream; if it isn't, bring to a simmer and reduce to the right consistency. When rabbit is cool enough to handle, pull the meat from the bones in large chunks, then stir meat back into sauce and keep warm until ready to serve.

Heat a small frying pan over medium heat, add butter and, when melted, add chestnuts and cook for a few minutes until heated through.

Bring a large saucepan of water to the boil, add fine sea salt, then pasta and boil for about 3 minutes from the time the water returns to the boil, until tender. Drain well, reserving some of the cooking water.

Add pasta to the sauce and toss for a minute or two to coat well. If it seems a bit dry, add a couple of tablespoons of reserved cooking water and stir it through well, adding a little more if necessary to give a creamy consistency. Serve in pasta bowls, topped with chestnuts, pecorino and a drizzle of olive oil.

HARE BRAISED IN MIRTO

LEPRE BRASATA CON MIRTO

SERVES 4

1 hare, skinned, gutted and head removed
plain flour, for dusting
⅓ cup (80 ml) vegetable oil
50 g butter
2 bulbs baby fennel, washed well
   and diced
4 stalks celery heart, diced
1 golden shallot, diced
6 cloves garlic, finely sliced
150 ml Cannonau (see page 219)
   or other full-bodied red wine
2 sprigs rosemary
2 litres Chicken Stock (see page 214)
salt flakes and freshly ground black
   pepper, to taste
Polenta (see page 128), for serving
fresh bay leaves, for garnishing

MIRTO MARINADE

300 ml red mirto
4 cloves garlic, peeled and bruised
8 bay leaves
10 juniper berries
freshly ground black pepper, to taste

In Sardinia, myrtle leaves are used in the marinade for the hare and as a garnish. If you happen to have a true myrtle tree in your yard (not lemon myrtle or crepe myrtle), use some of its leaves in place of the bay leaves here. For this recipe you'll need a large flameproof casserole wide enough to hold the hare pieces in a single layer, and you'll need to start 1–2 days ahead to give the hare time to marinate.

Joint hare as follows (or ask your butcher to do this for you): 2 front legs; 2 back legs, each halved to give lower leg and thigh joints; 2 belly flaps; rib cage, halved through the back bone; and the loin, cut into 3 pieces.

For the mirto marinade, combine all ingredients in a shallow glass or ceramic dish. Add hare, cover and refrigerate for 24–48 hours, turning occasionally.

Remove hare from fridge 1 hour before cooking. Set aside in a cool place to come to room temperature.

Remove hare pieces from marinade and pat dry, reserving marinade. Dust pieces in flour, shaking off any excess. Place a large flameproof casserole over high heat and add oil and butter. When butter starts to brown, reduce heat to medium, add hare and cook, in batches if necessary, until well browned on all sides, about 5 minutes. Remove and set aside on paper towel to drain.

Discard any dark bits of flour in the casserole. Add fennel, celery, shallot and garlic and cook over medium heat for about 5 minutes, stirring often, until soft and slightly coloured. Add reserved marinade, wine and rosemary, bring to the boil and cook for a few minutes until reduced by half. Add stock and salt, return to the boil, then reduce heat to lowest setting, add pieces of hare in a single layer, cover loosely with foil and simmer for 2–2½ hours, turning occasionally, until the meat is falling off the bone. Uncover and simmer for a further 10 minutes, then remove meat and cover to keep warm. Increase heat and boil sauce for about 30 minutes until reduced by half. Add salt and pepper and return hare to sauce to warm through.

Place polenta on a platter, arrange hare on top, pour sauce over, garnish with bay leaves and serve.

Mirto

Mirto is a bittersweet liqueur made from myrtle, which grows wild all over Sardinia. White mirto (*mirto bianco*) is made from the leaves and stems, while the more common red mirto (*mirto rosso*) is made from the berries. Traditionally it is sweetened with honey, though today sugar is also used. It's popular as a digestive at the end of a meal and is also used in desserts and savoury dishes. For details of where to buy mirto, see page 219.

WILD BOAR STEW

SPEZZATINO DI CINGHIALE

SERVES 6

500 g boar neck
500 g deboned boar shoulder
plain flour, for dusting
⅓ cup (80 ml) extra virgin olive oil
1 small brown onion, diced
2 cloves garlic, finely sliced
¼ teaspoon dried chilli flakes
3 bay leaves
20 Bosane olives (see page 219)
2 spunta potatoes, peeled
   and cut into 5 cm dice
salt flakes, to taste
crusty bread, for serving

RED WINE MARINADE

1 litre Cannonau (see page 219)
   or other full-bodied red wine
1 stalk celery, roughly chopped
1 brown onion, roughly chopped
1 carrot, roughly chopped
1 small bunch marjoram
1 small bunch oregano
4 sprigs rosemary

This dish is traditionally made with either the shoulder or the belly; my father always uses the belly because he loves the fat, but other people prefer the shoulder. Boar belly is hard to get unless you kill your own boar, so I've used a mixture of shoulder and neck here – though you will still have to order these in advance from your butcher. You'll need to start this recipe a day ahead to give the meat time to marinate. As the boar hunting season is during the colder months, Winter Salad (shown in the photo here; see page 64) makes a perfect accompaniment.

To make the red wine marinade, combine all ingredients in a glass or ceramic bowl.

Trim excess fat and connective tissue from boar, then cut into 5 cm dice and add to bowl, mixing well. Cover and refrigerate overnight.

Remove boar from fridge 1–2 hours before cooking. Set aside in a cool place to come to room temperature.

Drain the meat, reserving the marinade, and pat dry. Strain the marinade, discarding the solids and keeping the liquid. Dust meat with flour, shaking off any excess.

Heat a frying pan over high heat, add oil and, when hot, add meat and cook, in batches if necessary, until well browned on all sides, about 10 minutes. Stir in onion, garlic, chilli and bay leaves and cook for a couple of minutes. Add olives and enough of the reserved marinade to just cover the meat. Stir well to remove any bits stuck to the base and sides of the pan.

Bring to the boil, then reduce heat to its lowest setting and simmer, partially covered, for 1 hour, adding more marinade a little at a time as it starts to dry out. You may need to add a little water if all the marinade is used – the stew should be quite wet and saucy.

Add potato and salt and cook for a further hour or so, until meat is tender and a wooden skewer can be inserted into potato without any resistance. Remove from heat, cover and set aside to rest for 15 minutes.

Serve with crusty bread.

HUNTING WILD BOAR

I remember when I was eighteen and went hunting with my gun licence for the first time. I killed a boar on my first day and my mother was so proud she gave me 100,000 lira and said she'd give me another 100,000 if I killed another one next weekend – next weekend I killed two!

We hunt in teams, with the *capo caccia* as the head of the team. He has the experience and knows the strategy, placing people like players on a football field. We start to climb up the mountain, and the older men always send the younger ones right up to the top because they're the fittest. The older guys, including the grandfathers, stay down closer to the cars, where the food and wine is, and you're stuck up in the hills with your gun – nervously watching and waiting.

My father was always the one with the dogs – he and Zio (Uncle) Francesco always had the best dogs around. The boars are on a certain section of the hill and you have to try to enclose the area and surround the boars. The four or five guys with the dogs come in from one side to drive the boars up or down the hill, towards the *poste*, the men that are positioned to shoot them. The places where the boar is likely to break through or hide are named, so the *capo caccia* tells the guys, 'Go up the hill to the "white rock"' or 'Head to the "goat passage"'. He has to know who to put in the most difficult spots.

The first time I killed a boar there was a gap in the bushes about two metres wide. You hear him coming and you're so pumped up and you have to anticipate because he's so fast – you can't wait until you see him to shoot. You have to shoot ahead of him, so that by the time he reaches the bullet, it hits him. And then you walk back down the hill, to where the older men are already eating and drinking – and they see you, with a wild boar over your shoulders, and your father is so proud. It's such a big deal.

It's a competition, with each village keen to kill the most boars. Some hunters are particularly lucky, but it's all about destiny. You can't show off, or the luck will turn against you; if you're successful, you call it luck and act humbly – you don't boast. The whole thing is very superstitious.

After the hunt you bring the boar back to a common place, like the church hall, to cut it up and share it around. I remember my father always wanted the belly, because it was the tastiest cut. The boar-hunting season lasts for three months and my father still hunts every week during the season.

TROUT WITH WHITE WINE AND ROSEMARY

TROTA ALLA VERNACCIA E ROSMARINO

SERVES 4

4 × 300 g rainbow trout, gilled and gutted
1 salad onion, finely sliced
2 cloves garlic, finely sliced
2 sprigs rosemary, leaves finely chopped
20 Bosane olives (see page 219),
   cheeks cut from the pit
4 bay leaves
1 cup (250 ml) Vernaccia di Oristano
   (see page 219) or other dry white wine
2 tablespoons finely sliced flat-leaf
   parsley leaves
salt flakes and freshly ground black
   pepper, to taste
extra virgin olive oil, for drizzling

As kids we'd often stay out late at night in the hills around my village, catching trout in the streams. We'd run an electrical lead into the water from a makeshift generator (made using a modified pushbike dynamo) and stun the fish, which would just float to the surface – I don't recommend you try this, however, as I have heard of people being electrocuted doing it! This recipe is a classic way of cooking smaller fish, so buy the smallest trout you can find. If they were small enough, we'd often cook them with the gut still in, though this imparts a stronger flavour that may be an acquired taste. Grilled Mixed Vegetables (see page 61) are a perfect accompaniment, but you could also serve the fish with a simple salad.

Wash trout inside and out to remove slime from the skin and any blood from the belly cavity; pat dry.

Preheat oven to 180°C.

Lay fish on a chopping board and score on one side only, making 4 diagonal cuts just through to the bone.

Place fish on a baking tray, scored-side up. Scatter onion, garlic, rosemary and olives over the top and place a bay leaf on each fish. Pour wine over the fish and sprinkle with parsley, salt and quite a lot of pepper.

Cook in oven for 20–30 minutes, basting well at least every 10 minutes; check the flesh inside the scoring at the thickest part of the fish, it should be just opaque all the way to the bone. Remove from oven and place fish on plates.

Pour cooking juices into a small saucepan and simmer until slightly reduced, then spoon over fish. Drizzle with olive oil and serve.

Note

Whole fish should always be plated with their head to the left and their belly facing the diner – otherwise they look like they are swimming in the wrong direction.

TONNARELLI PASTA WITH SMOKED EEL AND SQUID

TONNARELLI CON ANGUILLA AFFUMICATA E CALAMARI

SERVES 6 AS A FIRST COURSE

½ quantity Fresh Pasta Dough #1
  (see page 217), passed through pasta
  machine four times
tipo oo flour, for dusting
100 g smoked eel, skinned and boned
300 g squid, cleaned and skinned
⅓ cup (80 ml) extra virgin olive oil
1 small clove garlic, finely sliced
1 small red chilli, finely sliced
¾ cup (180 ml) Prawn Stock (see page 213)
fine sea salt, for pasta water
50 g butter, diced
1½ tablespoons finely sliced chives
salt flakes, to taste

As kids we used to catch eels in the local creek: I'd wade into the stony creek bed to about ankle depth with three or four of my friends, then we'd all slide our hands under the rocks and feel for eels hiding beneath the stones. When we found one, someone would block the eel's exit, forcing it to swim towards us, and whoever the eel got closest to would quickly grab it and throw it up onto the river bank. Tonnarelli is a square spaghetti, similar to spaghetti alla chitarra; if you don't want to make fresh pasta, you can use 500 g dried spaghetti. Smoked eel is available from some fishmongers. If it's unavailable, substitute any hot-smoked fish, such as trout.

Cut pasta sheets into 24 cm lengths and trim the sides. Pass sheets through a spaghetti attachment on the pasta machine (see note). Toss with a little flour and set aside.

Cut eel into 1 cm dice. Cut squid hoods open. Using the back of a knife, scrape off the membrane from inside the hoods. Trim off the base and slice the hoods into thin strips; halve tentacles.

Bring a large saucepan of water to the boil.

Meanwhile, heat a frying pan, add oil and, when hot, add squid and cook for about 3 minutes until it turns opaque. Add garlic and chilli and cook for 1 minute. Add eel and stock, bring to the boil, then reduce heat and simmer for 5 minutes.

While the eel is cooking, add fine sea salt to the boiling water, add pasta and boil for about 3 minutes from the time the water returns to the boil, until tender.

Remove frying pan from heat and, using tongs or a spaghetti spoon, lift the cooked pasta from the boiling water into the frying pan. Toss pasta for a minute or two to coat well, adding a couple of tablespoons of the cooking water if it seems a bit dry. Add butter and toss it through, adding a little more cooking water if necessary to give a creamy consistency. Stir through chives and salt flakes and serve in pasta bowls.

Note
You'll need a spaghetti attachment for your pasta machine to make this pasta. If you don't have the correct attachment, you can fold the dough up into a flattened roll and cut into fine strips with a knife, but this takes a very sharp knife and a lot of practice to master.

NETTLE TAGLIOLINI WITH PECORINO, BLACK PEPPER AND CURED PORK CHEEK

TAGLIOLINI ALLE ORTICHE 'CACIO E PEPE' E GUANCIALE

SERVES 4 AS A FIRST COURSE

1 quantity Pasta Dough #3 (see page 217)
    made with nettle purée (see below) and
    passed through pasta machine five times
tipo oo flour, for dusting
2 tablespoons extra virgin olive oil
160 g guanciale (see page 220), diced
fine sea salt, for pasta water
freshly ground black pepper, to taste
120 g aged Pecorino Sardo, freshly grated
50 g butter, diced

NETTLE PURÉE

500 g nettles
200 ml Vermentino (see page 219)
    or other dry white wine
pinch dried chilli flakes
2 cloves garlic, peeled and bruised
6 black peppercorns
salt flakes, to taste

Notes

Any leftover nettle purée can be frozen;
it's great stirred through a plain risotto
(start with about 1 teaspoon per person
and add more to taste).

You'll need a tagliolini attachment for
your pasta machine to make this pasta;
if you don't have the correct attachment,
use the thinnest attachment you have.
Traditionally, the dough is folded up into
a flattened roll and cut into fine strips
with a knife, but this takes a very sharp
knife and a lot of practice to master.

Nettles aren't called stinging nettles for nothing (if they come into contact with your skin, you'll be left with an itchy rash that can last for days), so be careful when handling them and always wear rubber gloves; cooking them removes the stinging element. If harvesting nettles from the wild, pick only the young shoots and tops of the nettles. Nettles are widely available from greengrocers these days, though you may have to order them in advance, but you still need to pick over them and discard the coarse stems. If nettles are unavailable, you can make this dish with other greens, such as spinach. *Cacio e pepe*, a classic Roman sauce, is one of my favourites, but of course I use Pecorino Sardo instead of Pecorino Romano! You'll need a tagliolini attachment for your pasta machine.

First make the nettle purée. Wearing gloves, pick the leaves off the nettles, discarding the stems. Place wine, chilli, garlic, peppercorns, salt and 1 litre of water in a saucepan and bring to the boil. Add nettle leaves and cook for 3 minutes, then drain, reserving the water.

Place nettles in a food processor and blend, adding 1–2 tablespoons of reserved cooking water, if necessary, to make a smooth paste. Pass through a fine sieve. Measure 50 ml of the purée and set this aside; the rest can be frozen for later use (see notes). Use this purée to make the pasta dough (see page 217).

Pass pasta sheets through a tagliolini attachment on the pasta machine. Toss with a little flour and set aside.

Bring a large saucepan of water to the boil.

Meanwhile, heat a frying pan, add oil and, when hot, add guanciale and cook over medium heat until crisp.

Add salt to boiling water, gently shake tagliolini to loosen it a little, then drop it into the water and boil for about 1 minute from the time the water returns to the boil, until tender.

Remove frying pan from heat and, using tongs or a spaghetti spoon, lift the cooked pasta from the boiling water into the frying pan. Toss pasta for a minute or two to coat well with guanciale and oil. Grind in plenty of pepper and toss again, then mix in three-quarters of the pecorino, followed by the butter. Add about ½ cup (125 ml) of the pasta cooking water and toss thoroughly to give a creamy consistency, adding a little more water if it seems too dry.

Serve in pasta bowls, topped with the remaining pecorino and a good grind of pepper.

Pastries and Desserts

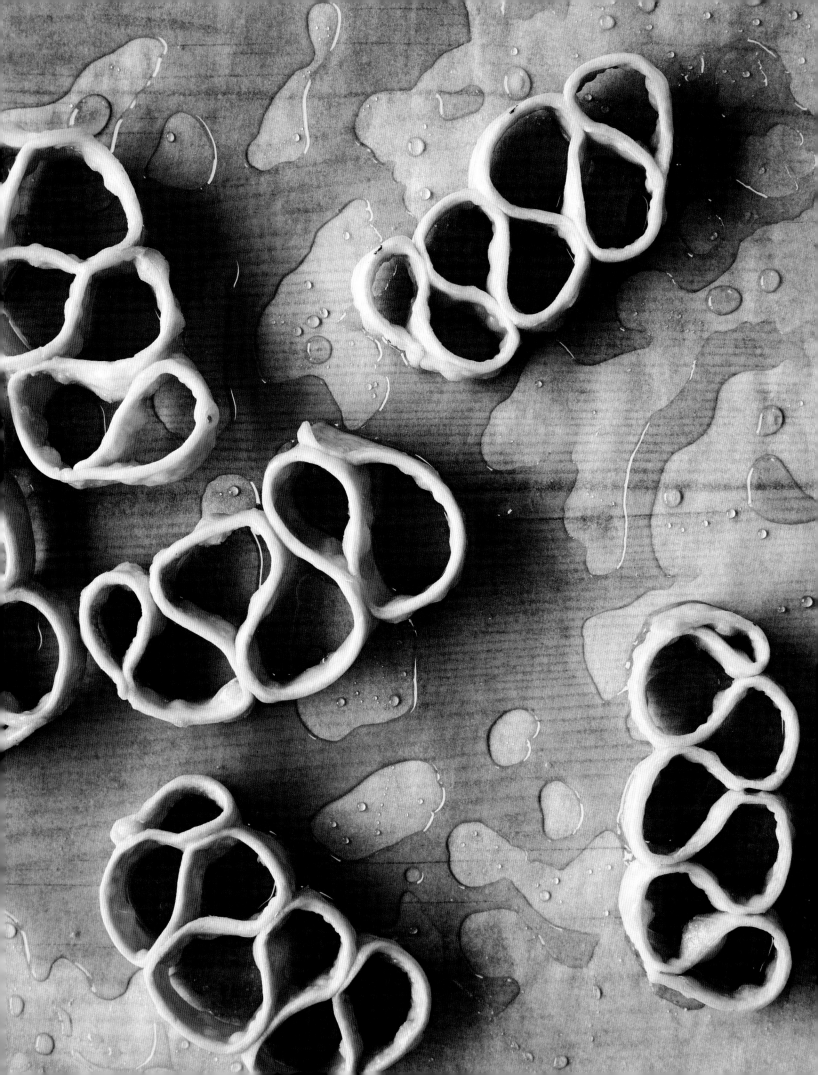

ost of Sardinia's traditional desserts are baked. There are many biscuits and sweets that are only made once a year for festivals and other special occasions such as Christmas, Easter and All Saints Day (*Tutti i Santi* on 1 November), like the wonderful *frisciolas* (see page 172), saffron and potato doughnuts made for Carnevale. These are something to look forward to, a way of marking the passing of the seasons and the cycles of the year.

The Arabic influence is obvious in many Sardinian sweets, with lots of recipes using almonds, which were introduced by the Arabs; dried fruits, citrus zest and other nuts are also common. Like Arabic sweetmeats, they're often very sweet, topped with honey or syrup, and usually served as small bites, in many different shapes. As you'll have seen by now, nothing is ever wasted, and so the grape skins and pips left over when the grapes are pressed to make wine ('must', or *mosto* in Italian) is boiled down to make a syrup called *saba*, which is often used in desserts or baking. The influence of other invaders, such as the Catalans, is seen in sweet treats such as *crema Catalana* (see page 184) and *chidonzada*, or quince paste.

Sardinia doesn't have a strong tradition of eating dessert as such; meals often end with some pecorino or a coffee and mirto liqueur (see page 153), or a piece of fruit. Biscuits are usually served on a special occasion – mind you, a friend or neighbour dropping by for a visit is a special enough occasion to bring them out. In restaurants and for special family meals, a big, colourful basket of sweets (*cestino di dolci*) is always brought out after dinner.

See also
- Ricotta and Pecorino Tarts (page 196) in 'Cheese and Drinks'
- Ricotta Cake with Walnuts, Almonds and Candied Orange (page 200) in 'Cheese and Drinks'
- Deep-fried Cheese Pastries (page 202) in 'Cheese and Drinks'
- Ricotta Fritters with Honey (page 204) in 'Cheese and Drinks'
- Quince Paste (page 207) in 'Cheese and Drinks'

CHERRIES POACHED IN MIRTO WITH SHEEP'S MILK YOGHURT ICE CREAM

CILIEGIE IN CAMICIA AL MIRTO CON GELATO ALLO YOGURT DI LATTE DI PECORA

SERVES 4

500 g cherries
1 cup (220 g) castor sugar
¼ cup (60 ml) red mirto (see page 153)
1 cinnamon stick
1 bay leaf

SHEEP'S MILK YOGHURT ICE CREAM

1 cup (250 ml) pouring cream
70 ml full-cream milk
75 g castor sugar
30 g invert sugar
50 g liquid glucose
45 g dried milk powder
250 g sheep's milk yoghurt

Fruit is often poached in mirto, Sardinia's national liqueur. This dish is perfect in summer when cherries are in season and gelato is always welcome. You'll need an ice cream machine to make this, as the result should be silky smooth. Sponge Finger Biscuits (see page 186) make a great accompaniment.

To make the ice cream, combine cream, milk, castor sugar, invert sugar and glucose in a saucepan and stir over medium heat until sugar dissolves. Bring to the boil, then immediately remove from the heat and scatter in milk powder, whisking constantly until dissolved. Pass through a fine sieve into a bowl and set aside, stirring occasionally to help it cool more quickly. When cool, whisk in yoghurt. Place mixture in an ice cream machine and churn according to manufacturer's instructions. Freeze until needed.

Remove stalks and pits from cherries. Combine sugar, mirto, cinnamon, bay leaf and ½ cup (125 ml) of water in a large saucepan and stir over medium heat until sugar dissolves. Add cherries, cover and bring to the boil. Remove from the heat and set aside to cool in the syrup.

Divide cherries among serving bowls, drizzle with the syrup and top with a scoop of ice cream.

Note

Invert sugar (also called trimoline) is a mixture of glucose and fructose. Sweeter than regular sugar, it also helps prevent ice cream from crystallising, giving a smoother result. It's available from specialist confectionery suppliers or can be easily made at home. Combine 1 kg castor sugar, 480 ml water and ¼ teaspoon cream of tartar or citric acid in a non-reactive saucepan. Bring to the boil, stirring constantly, then wash away any sugar crystals stuck to the side of the pan with a pastry brush dipped in water. Reduce heat to medium and, without stirring, boil the syrup until it registers 114°C on a sugar thermometer (this needs to be fairly precise – if this temperature is exceeded, a thin layer of sugar crystals may form on top of the cooled invert sugar). Remove from heat, cover, and leave to cool at room temperature. Don't try making a smaller quantity than this – any extra can be stored in the fridge for 6 months. You could also substituted honey or light corn syrup for the invert sugar, but the texture won't be as smooth and honey will of course give a different flavour.

PANNA COTTA WITH HONEYCOMB SAUCE

PANNA COTTA ALL'ABBAMELE

SERVES 6

2 leaves titanium-strength gelatine
500 ml pouring cream
½ cup (125 ml) full-cream milk
100 g castor sugar
½ vanilla bean
non-stick cooking spray
candied orange slices, for serving

ABBAMELE

1 kg honeycomb
¼ cup (60 ml) strained orange juice
¼ cup (60 ml) strained lemon juice
rind of 1 lemon, in large strips,
   white pith removed
rind of 1 orange, in large strips,
   white pith removed

Abbamele is a traditional Sardinian product (see page 177); it's great with ricotta on toast for breakfast and is often used in desserts. It's worth making a big batch because it keeps for ages – just be careful when skimming and straining it as the molten honey will be very hot. You'll need a thermometer to make the panna cotta, which is set in the fridge overnight.

To make the abbamele, place honeycomb, citrus juices and rinds in a very large saucepan over low heat and cook for about 20 minutes, until honeycomb has completely melted, skimming off the wax as it floats to the top. Bring to the boil, then reduce heat and simmer for about 1½ hours, skimming regularly to remove any froth that rises to the surface. Strain into a clean bowl.

For the panna cotta, soak gelatine in cold water for about 5 minutes. Meanwhile, place cream, milk, sugar and vanilla bean in a saucepan and heat to 85°C. Squeeze gelatine to remove excess water then stir through the cream mixture until dissolved. Pass through a fine sieve. Split vanilla bean and scrape seeds into the mixture.

Spray six 150 ml plastic dariole moulds with non-stick spray. Pour 1 tablespoon of abbamele into each mould. Fill moulds with cream mixture and refrigerate for 24 hours.

Turn moulds upside down over plates and squeeze gently to loosen; if panna cotta doesn't slide out, ease a butter knife between the panna cotta and the side of the mould to break the seal. Serve with candied orange slices.

Notes

Different brands and grades of gelatine leaves have different setting strengths. The amounts given in this recipe are for Gelita brand titanium-strength leaves, which are the most commonly seen; they're available from some delicatessens and speciality food shops.

Honeycomb is available from some delicatessens, as is candied orange.

Abbamele keeps for months stored in an airtight container in a cool place.

SAFFRON AND POTATO DOUGHNUTS

FRISCIOLAS

MAKES ABOUT 30

100 g desiree potato (about 1 small potato)
½ cup (125 ml) full-cream milk
¼ teaspoon saffron threads
35 g fresh yeast *or* 17.5 g dried yeast
1 cup (220 g) castor sugar
450 g plain flour, plus extra for dusting
pinch fine sea salt
juice and finely grated zest of 2 oranges
1 egg, lightly beaten
50 ml grappa
vegetable oil, for deep-frying
mascarpone, for serving

Note

If you don't have a potato ricer, you'll need to peel the potato before mashing it.

These sweets are traditionally made for the celebrations of Carnevale, which runs from *Giovedi Grasso* ('fat Thursday'), the Thursday before Lent, to *Martedi Grasso* ('fat Tuesday', *Mardi Gras* in French), the day before the Lenten fast begins. I remember my aunties shaping *frisciolas* like doughnuts with a hole in the middle, but they're made in different shapes all over Italy. *Frisciolas* is the name for them in my dad's dialect, but Mum calls them *cattas*, and they're also known as *zippulas* and *frittelle*. At the restaurant we zest the oranges with a citrus zester, mix it with the sugar, spread it out on a tray and leave it overnight to dry, then pound it lightly; this produces a lovely orange-scented sugar to coat the *frisciolas*. This recipe makes a lot, but you can't easily halve an egg – and the doughnuts are light, easy to eat and make great snacks; they keep well for a few days in an airtight container.

Put the unpeeled potato in a saucepan of salted water, and cook until a wooden skewer can be inserted without any resistance, about 20 minutes. Drain well, then press through a potato ricer onto a plate and spread out to cool completely.

Place milk and saffron in a small saucepan and heat until just simmering. Remove from heat and set aside, whisking occasionally, until the milk has cooled to lukewarm, about 40°C. Add yeast to milk with a pinch of sugar and whisk until yeast is dissolved. Set aside for 5–10 minutes.

Sift flour and salt into a large bowl, make a well in the centre and pour in orange juice, egg, potato, grappa and milk mixture. Using a fork, mix the flour into the liquid until combined, then knead by hand to form a soft, sticky dough. Transfer to a clean, lightly floured workbench and knead lightly for a few minutes, dusting with a little more flour if the dough is too sticky to handle – it should be smooth, elastic and slightly sticky.

Place the dough in an oiled bowl and smear a little oil over the top. Cover with plastic wrap and set aside in a warm place for 1–2 hours, until the dough has doubled in size.

Dust a baking tray with flour and, using floured hands, break off walnut-sized pieces of dough and roll into balls. Place on tray, cover loosely with plastic wrap and set aside for 10–20 minutes, until they've risen to about 1½ times their original size.

Combine orange zest and remaining sugar well in a shallow bowl.

Heat vegetable oil to 160°C (if you don't have a deep-frying thermometer, test the temperature of the oil by dipping the handle of a wooden spoon into it – when bubbles form around the spoon, the oil is hot enough). Lower dough balls carefully into hot oil, 3 or 4 at a time, and deep-fry until underside is golden brown and crisp, then turn and fry other side.

Drain doughnuts on paper towel and toss in orange-scented sugar while still hot. Serve with mascarpone.

FRIED PASTRY LOOPS WITH HONEY

ORIGLIETTAS

MAKES ABOUT 30

125 g tipo oo flour, plus extra for dusting
125 g bread flour
pinch fine sea salt
10 egg yolks, lightly beaten
1 teaspoon melted duck fat, lard or butter
vegetable oil, for shallow-frying
400 g honey

My cousin Rina is the expert at making these pastries, which are meant to be biscuity without being soggy. They can be fried then stored in an airtight container for up to 4 days before being dipped in honey and eaten. Traditionally they're served stacked up in a big mound – make sure they're completely cold before stacking them or they'll stick together. Lard would traditionally have been used in the dough and also to fry the pastries, because that's what was available, but butter or duck fat work just as well in the dough.

Sift both flours and salt into the bowl of an electric mixer fitted with a dough hook. With the machine running, pour in three-quarters of the egg yolk and mix until absorbed, then mix in the duck fat, lard or butter. If the mixture is still too dry to form a dough, start adding remaining egg yolk, a little at a time, to form a rough dough. You may not need it all; towards the end, it doesn't take much extra liquid for the dough to become too soft. Tip the dough onto a clean, lightly floured workbench and knead with the heels of your hands for about 5 minutes, until smooth and elastic. Roll into a ball, wrap in plastic wrap and set aside for about 30 minutes.

Cut dough into two pieces and flatten one slightly, re-wrapping the other one in plastic wrap to prevent it drying out. Pass the flattened dough through a pasta machine on the widest setting, then fold in half and pass through the machine again. Repeat the folding and passing twice more. Reduce the setting on the machine a notch and pass the dough through. Repeat twice more, reducing the setting each time; dust the dough lightly with flour if it starts to stick.

Turn the setting on the pasta machine back to the widest one, fold dough sheet in thirds (like a brochure) and pass through the machine again. Pass the dough through twice more, reducing the setting each time. Fold sheet in thirds again, rotate 90 degrees, turn the setting back to the widest and pass through the machine six times, reducing the setting each time. When the dough gets too long to handle, cut it in half and continue with each half separately; if it becomes too long to handle again, cut in half again. By now, the pastry should be about 2 mm thick and fine enough that you can see your hand through it. Repeat with remaining piece of dough.

Lay a sheet of pastry on a clean, lightly floured workbench and, using a wheel pastry cutter, cut into strips 1 cm wide and at least 40 cm long. Stand a strip on its side and fold the end to form a loop, squeezing the end of the loop to hold it in place; if the pastry won't stick, wet your finger with a drop of water and dab it on the pastry. Fold the pastry back in the opposite direction to form another loop and squeeze the end to hold it in place. Continue folding and squeezing in this way until you reach the end of the strip. Place on a lightly floured tray and repeat with remaining pastry.

Meanwhile, pour a 2 cm depth of vegetable oil into a frying pan and heat to 160°C (if you don't have a thermometer, test the temperature of the oil by dipping the handle of a wooden spoon into it – when bubbles form around the spoon, the oil is hot enough). Place several pastries in the hot oil, being careful not to overcrowd the pan; they'll puff up almost immediately. Fry on one side for about 30 seconds until lightly golden, then turn using an egg lifter and a fork and fry the other side for another 30 seconds. Drain on paper towel and repeat with remaining pastries.

When pastries are cool, line several trays with baking paper. Heat honey in a medium-sized saucepan until almost boiling, then reduce heat to its lowest setting. Carefully lower a pastry into the honey and, using an egg lifter and a fork, gently turn it over, then lift it out and place on a tray to cool. Repeat with remaining pastries.

HONEY

Honey was Sardinia's original sweetener, collected from wild hives and used instead of expensive imported sugar.

The most common honey is still *millefiori* ('thousand flowers'), collected from the hives of bees that have roamed around fields of wild flowers. But there are also many different types of honey derived from the flowers of specific plants that are used for their distinctive flavours, including eucalyptus, acacia, chestnut, lavender, rosemary and cardoon. The most classically Sardinian of these comes from the flowers of *corbezzolo*, or 'wild strawberry', a tree which grows wild all over the island. Called *miele amaro* (bitter honey), it has a complex flavour, starting slightly sweet with a long, pleasantly bitter aftertaste. By October, when the tree flowers, the bees are at the end of their honey-making season and so there's only a short window of time for them to gather the nectar from the small white, bell-shaped flower and produce this highly prized honey.

Abbamele is a Sardinian dialect word that comes from *abba*, meaning 'water', and *mele*, meaning 'honey'. This distinctively Sardinian product is traditionally made by boiling whole honeycomb with citrus zest and water to extract both the honey and the pollen, producing a thick amber syrup with a caremelly flavour (see page 171). As well as being used in many Sardinian desserts, it's often drizzled over cheese.

ALMOND NOUGAT

TORRONE ALLE MANDORLE

MAKES ABOUT 40 PIECES

4 sheets rice paper
1 egg white
pinch fine sea salt
300 g castor sugar
175 g honey
2 tablespoons water
300 g unpeeled almonds,
   lightly toasted (see page 222)

Introduced by the Arabs, almond trees are very common in Sardinia, and in spring the white almond blossom is a breathtaking sight. I remember being at my grandfather's house as a kid at Eastertime, spending the morning cracking almonds to make meringues, nougat and other sweets. We'd sit around on the steps cracking the almonds and fighting over the hammer. There were never enough hammers for everyone, and the smaller children who couldn't get their hands on a hammer would hit the side of the almond with a stone to crack the shell without crushing the almond kernel inside. This recipe for traditional nougat makes the most of fresh almonds – you'll need a sugar thermometer to make the nougat.

Lay two sheets of rice paper, slightly overlapping, on a baking tray to form a rectangle about 24 cm × 15 cm.

Using an electric mixer, whisk egg white and salt in a heatproof bowl until stiff peaks form.

Combine sugar, honey and water in a saucepan and cook over medium heat until it reaches 126–8°C.

With the mixer on low speed, slowly pour the sugar mixture into the egg white. Once all the sugar is added, increase speed and whisk until the mixture doubles in size. Fold in almonds while mixture is still warm, then pour onto the centre of the rice paper. Top with remaining sheets of rice paper, slightly overlapping them.

Using a rolling pin, gently roll the mound of nougat so that it spreads evenly, forming a 1 cm thick layer of nougat between the top and bottom sheets of rice paper.

Leave to cool to room temperature, then trim edges and cut into 3 cm squares or diamonds, using a sharp knife dipped in hot water.

Store in an airtight container in a cool place for up to a week, but do not refrigerate or it will soften and become sticky.

Note

The rice paper needed for this dish, also called edible wafer paper, is available from the baking section of specialist stores and some delicatessens; it's not the same as the rice paper found in Asian grocery stores that's used for making spring rolls.

ALMOND MERINGUES

BIANCHINI

MAKES ABOUT 30

185 g egg white (from 6–7 eggs)
pinch fine sea salt
350 g castor sugar
150 g blanched almonds, toasted
   (see page 222) and roughly chopped
finely grated zest of 1 lemon

This is another almond recipe for Eastertime, when the almonds are fresh. I remember my aunties make *bianchini*: as they had no electric mixers, not even a whisk, they'd whip the mixture using two forks, passing the bowl between them as each one tired. All the kids watched and waited, hoping to get a chance to lick the bowl. After lunch, my aunties would cook these in the wood-fired oven, which my father had lit the day before. By lunchtime the next day the temperature would be right; there weren't any thermostats, and the oven temperature was crucial, but they knew from experience when it was just right. Sometimes these almond meringues are decorated with hundreds and thousands.

Using an electric mixer, whisk egg white and salt until frothy. With the mixer on low speed, slowly pour the sugar into the egg white and whisk until stiff peaks form. Fold through the almonds and lemon zest.

Preheat oven to 100°C. Lightly brush a baking tray with water, then line with baking paper.

Scoop up a dessertspoon of the meringue mixture and, using a second spoon, scrape it onto the tray to form a rough blob. Continue until all the mixture is used, leaving about 1 cm between the meringues.

Cook the meringues in the oven for about 2 hours, until they're crusty on the outside but still slightly soft inside.

Remove from oven and leave on the tray until cool. Store in an airtight container for up to 2 weeks.

*Clockwise from bottom left:
Diamond Biscuits (page 183);
Almond Bonbons (page 182),
wrapped in paper; Almond
Meringues (this page)*

Note

You'll need six or seven 55 g eggs to get enough egg white for this recipe; it's important that you weigh the whites to get as close as possible to the exact weight.

ALMOND BONBONS

SOSPIROS

MAKES ABOUT 25 PIECES

1 tablespoon orange blossom water
1½ cups (330 g) castor sugar
1 cup (160 g) blanched almonds, toasted
(see page 222) and finely ground

A large basket of sweets (*cestino di dolci*), including these treats wrapped in colourful paper, is generally offered to guests with coffee. If you want to do this, wrap the cooled sweets in rectangles of different-coloured tissue paper, twisting the ends to form bonbons (as in the photo on page 180).

Place orange blossom water and 1 cup (220 g) of the sugar in a saucepan and cook over low heat until sugar is dissolved. Increase heat to medium, add almonds and stir constantly until the mixture comes away from the side of the pan and forms a ball, about 5–10 minutes. Remove from heat and set aside.

Place remaining castor sugar in a bowl.

When mixture is cool enough to handle, pull off pieces and roll into bite-sized balls. Toss in castor sugar then set aside to cool completely.

If desired, wrap in coloured paper, twisting the ends like bonbons and snipping them to fan them out a little.

Notes

Orange blossom water is available from Middle Eastern grocery stores and some delicatessens.

Allow toasted almonds to cool, then pulse lightly in a food processor until finely ground; if you process them too much, the oil will separate and they will become dry and hard.

DIAMOND BISCUITS

PAPASSINI

MAKES ABOUT 22 PIECES

200 g sultanas
570 g plain flour
150 g castor sugar
pinch freshly grated nutmeg
150 g cold butter, diced
200 g slivered almonds
finely grated zest of 1 orange
finely grated zest of 1 lemon
100 g candied orange, diced
5 egg whites, lightly beaten
2 eggs, lightly beaten
hundreds and thousands, for sprinkling

LEMON GLAZE

2 tablespoons strained lemon juice
100 g pure icing sugar, sifted

These are another of the Sardinian sweets typically served in a big basket at the end of a meal (see photo on page 180); they're traditionally made with lard, but I've substituted butter. They're always cut into a diamond shape, then half are glazed with icing and sprinkled with hundreds and thousands and half are left plain; the children tend to go for the glazed ones, but the older people often prefer them unglazed. The name is derived from a dialect word for sultanas (*papassa*, which is related to the Italian *passito*, a wine made from dried grapes).

Preheat oven to 150°C and line two baking trays with baking paper.

Cover sultanas with warm water and set aside for about 30 minutes to reconstitute; drain and pat dry.

Sift flour into a bowl and mix in sugar and nutmeg. Using your fingers, rub in the butter. Fold in the sultanas, almonds, orange and lemon zests, candied orange, egg whites and eggs and knead to form a soft dough.

Lay a large piece of baking paper on a clean, dry workbench and place the dough on top. Top with another piece of baking paper and roll out to a 1 cm thick rectangle. Remove the top sheet of paper and, using a sharp knife dipped in boiling water, slice dough, on the diagonal, into 6 cm wide strips. Slice in the opposite direction, on the diagonal, to form diamond shapes, dipping the knife into the water often to prevent it sticking to the dough.

Place the diamond biscuits on the prepared baking trays. Reroll off-cuts, slice as above and place on trays. Cook in oven for 20 minutes, then swap the positions of the trays and cook for a further 20 minutes or so, until lightly browned.

Meanwhile, make the lemon glaze: beat half the lemon juice into the icing sugar to form a thin icing. If it's too thick to pour easily, add more lemon juice until it's thin enough. Set aside.

Remove biscuits from oven and place on a cooling rack with a sheet of baking paper on the bench underneath. When biscuits are cool, pour glaze over half of them, sprinkle with hundreds and thousands and set aside until glaze hardens. Serve glazed and unglazed biscuits together.

Notes
Candied orange is available from some delicatessens.

BAKED CUSTARD WITH TOFFEE CRUST

CREMA CATALANA

SERVES 6

This dish is another reminder of the Catalan and Spanish influence in Sardinia. It's a classic Catalan dessert that is equally popular in Sardinia; the shallow terracotta moulds traditionally used to make it are available from Spanish shops and some kitchenware stores. You need a small butane-powered blowtorch, also available from kitchenware stores, to make this dish.

SERVES 6

4 egg yolks
1 tablespoon cornflour
200 g castor sugar
2 cups (500 ml) full-cream milk
1 cinnamon stick
1 small piece lemon rind,
    white pith removed
¼ teaspoon saffron threads
1 vanilla bean, split
½ cup (110 g) demerara sugar
Sponge Finger Biscuits (see page 186),
    for serving

Using an electric mixer, beat egg yolks, cornflour and 150 g of the castor sugar until pale.

Combine milk, remaining castor sugar, cinnamon, lemon rind and saffron threads in a saucepan. Scrape the seeds from the vanilla bean into the saucepan, add the bean then bring the milk to a simmer. Remove cinnamon, lemon and vanilla bean.

With the machine running, slowly pour the hot milk over the egg mixture, mixing until smooth. Return custard mixture to a clean saucepan and heat over very low heat, stirring constantly, until custard thickens enough to coat the back of a wooden spoon. Pour into six 100 ml moulds and refrigerate for at least 3 hours, preferably overnight.

Sprinkle with demerara sugar and caramelise with a blowtorch, then serve with sponge finger biscuits.

Note
Demerara sugar is a natural brown sugar named after Demerara, a colony in what is now Guyana, where the sugar was originally produced. It's available in some supermarkets and delicatessens; if unavailable, use castor sugar.

SPONGE FINGER BISCUITS

SAVOIARDI

MAKES 25-30

5 eggs, separated, at room temperature
160 g castor sugar, plus extra
  for sprinkling
2 drops white wine vinegar
½ teaspoon vanilla extract
125 g plain flour
40 g rice flour
¼ teaspoon baking powder
pinch fine sea salt

These are named after the House of Savoy, which ruled Sardinia (and ultimately the kingdom of Italy) until the end of World War II, when Italy became a republic. In Sardinia, they're always served after a funeral with black coffee but also when guests come to visit. Guests are very important in Sardinia and whenever I make savoiardi, even today, they remind me of the excitement of having guests and serving them coffee and these biscuits.

Preheat oven to 220°C. Line two large baking trays with baking paper.

Using an electric mixer, beat the egg yolks with 3 tablespoons of the sugar in a large mixing bowl for 3–5 minutes, until the mixture is light and thick and forms a slowly dissolving ribbon when the beater is lifted. Set aside.

In a separate, warmed bowl, beat the egg whites at high speed with clean beaters until foamy. Gradually beat the remaining sugar into the egg whites, continue beating at high speed until they form stiff, shiny peaks. Beat in the vinegar and the vanilla. Set aside.

Sift flour, rice flour, baking powder and salt together.

Fold a quarter of the egg yolk mixture into the egg white mixture. Then, in about 5 batches, gently fold the flour mixture and the egg white mixture alternately into the remainder of the egg yolk mixture.

Spoon the batter into a piping bag fitted with a 2 cm plain tip and pipe 12 cm long strips of batter, about 3 cm apart, onto the prepared trays. Sprinkle generously with castor sugar and bake in oven for 10–15 minutes, until lightly golden.

Cool the biscuits on racks, then store in an airtight container for 2–3 weeks.

Note
Rice flour, a very fine flour made from ground rice, adds texture to biscuits and batters. It's sometime sold as ground rice and is available from most supermarkets; potato starch can be substituted.

PRICKLY PEAR SORBET

SORBETTO DI FICHI D'INDIA

SERVES 10

10 prickly pears
100 ml strained lemon juice
300 g castor sugar
1 cup (250 ml) water
½ teaspoon liquid glucose

Prickly pears (literally 'figs of India' in Italian) are the fruit of a cactus native to North America that was introduced to Europe in the 17th century. The cactus now grows wild all over the southern Mediterranean. In Sardinia rows of prickly pears were often planted to divide land – they make a good fence because they grow very large and you can't get past them because of the spikes. The land owners were the meanest: the fruit would fall on the ground and rot, but they wouldn't let anyone take it; as kids we'd go and steal them from the fields and if the owners were coming we'd rush to eat them, often getting the spikes in our hands and mouths. These spikes irritate the skin, so always wear gloves when handling them. (If you buy them from a greengrocer, they're usually already washed so that the spikes fall off, but it's still a good idea to wear gloves.) Sorbet made from prickly pears is a beautiful golden colour (as in the photo on page 188).

Wearing gloves, peel prickly pears: holding them on a cutting board with a fork, cut off the top and bottom and split the skin across the middle without cutting into the flesh. Use the knife to start peeling back the skin, then put the fork down and reach into the split with your first two fingers and thumb and scoop out the flesh, rolling it away from the skin while holding the skin in place with the knife.

Place flesh in a blender with lemon juice and process to a smooth purée. Pass through a fine sieve into a bowl.

Combine sugar, water and glucose in a small saucepan and stir over low heat until sugar dissolves. Remove from heat, and stir into the purée. Set aside to cool then churn in an ice cream machine according to manufacturer's instructions.

Sorbets

Sorbets (*sorbetti* in Italian) differ from ice cream or gelato in that they don't contain any dairy products. They often have quite an intense flavour and so are great served in small scoops as a palate cleanser or pre-dessert at the end of a meal, before the main dessert.

POMEGRANATE SORBET

SORBETTO DI MELOGRANO

SERVES 10

3–5 pomegranates, depending on size
juice of 1 lemon, strained
155 g castor sugar
155 ml water
1 teaspoon liquid glucose
2 teaspoons pomegranate molasses

Sometimes during the middle of the day, if our mothers let us out when we should have been resting, we'd go and steal pomegranates, prickly pears, cherries and whatever other fruit was in season while the farmers were having their *riposino* (midday naps). Between 1 and 4 p.m., the hottest part of the day, was the only time the farmers weren't in their fields, so we'd feast on as much fruit as we could, which in the heat of the day often left us feeling decidedly unwell, but it never stopped us! I remember there were two types of pomegranates – sweet and sour – if you accidentally stole a sour one, you ate it anyway because that's what you had and it was better than nothing.

Halve pomegranates, hold over a bowl and squeeze gently to loosen seeds. Tap skin with a spoon and most seeds will fall out, scoop out remaining seeds with a spoon. Place seeds in a blender with lemon juice and process until well combined. Pass through a fine sieve into a measuring jug; you'll need 350 ml juice for the sorbet, if there's any leftover, drink it (don't be tempted to add it to the sorbet or it may not set).

Combine sugar, water, glucose and pomegranate molasses in a small saucepan and stir over low heat until sugar dissolves. Remove from heat and whisk into the pomegranate juice. Set aside to cool then churn in an ice cream machine according to manufacturer's instructions.

In tall glasses:
Prickly Pear Sorbet (page 187);
in short glasses:
Pomegranate Sorbet (this page)

Note

Pomegranate molasses is made by boiling pomegranate juice down to a thick, dark syrup with a sweet-sour taste; it's available from Middle Eastern grocers and some delicatessens.

PEARS POACHED IN RED WINE WITH GINGER SEMIFREDDO

PERE COTTE AL CANNONAU CON SEMIFREDDO ALLO ZENZERO

SERVES 8

8 large corella pears
1 litre Cannonau (see page 219)
   or other full-bodied red wine
10 cloves
1 cinnamon stick, split
rind of 1 orange, in large strips,
   white pith removed
400 g castor sugar

GINGER SEMIFREDDO

6 egg yolks
150 g castor sugar
150 ml water
1 teaspoon freshly grated ginger
200 ml pouring cream, whipped

Pears look beautiful poached in red wine, as their pale flesh takes up the colour so well. I like to use large corella pears for this dish – they have a great texture and are just the right size for one per person. If they aren't available, use firm pears that weigh around 150 g each. Another remnant of the Arabic influence in Sardinia, ginger is most commonly used in the south of the island. You'll need to start this recipe a day ahead to give the semifreddo time to set.

For the ginger semifreddo, beat egg yolks in an electric mixer until well combined.

Place sugar and water in a small saucepan and bring to a rapid boil, then reduce heat and simmer for 4 minutes, stirring continuously. Slowly drizzle into egg mixture, whisking continuously, then whisk until cool, glossy, pale and tripled in volume.

Fold ginger through whipped cream. Add cream to egg mixture in 3 batches, gently folding in until just incorporated. Pour into a rectangular cake tin or plastic container, then cover and freeze for at least 6 hours, preferably overnight.

Trim the base off the pears and peel them, leaving stalks intact. Arrange pears in a single layer, standing upright, in a saucepan just large enough to hold them. Add wine, cloves, cinnamon, orange peel and sugar. Cover with a sheet of baking paper, tucking it in around the sides and pressing it onto the surface. Bring to the boil, then reduce heat and simmer for about 40 minutes, until a wooden skewer can be inserted into a pear without any resistance (avoiding the core). Remove pears, cover and set aside in a warm place.

Return poaching liquid to medium heat and boil for about 30 minutes, until reduced to a syrupy consistency, then strain.

Serve pears warm or at room temperature, with syrup drizzled over them and a scoop of semifreddo on the side.

MAGGi
VANDS

*Cheese and
Drinks*

As an island, Sardinia has many unique grape varieties, as well as a number introduced from Spain that have developed a distinctive style when grown in Sardinian terroir. Vermentino is Sardinia's most common white wine and Cannonau the most common red, but there are many others and, like those from other lesser known regions of Italy, Sardinia's wines are now starting to be noticed by the rest of the world. Production is dominated by large cooperatives, though most families still also make *il vino dello zio* ('uncle's wine') for personal consumption. (See page 209 for more information on Sardinian wines.)

Sardinian wines are still largely sealed under cork rather than screw caps, as cork trees grow all over the island. As well as being used to seal bottles of wine, olive oil and *saba*, cork is used to make platters (called *concheddu* in my dialect) which are traditionally used by shepherds as plates but now also popular in restaurants and as souvenirs. I use them at my restaurant to serve suckling pig (as in the photo on page 127).

Another distinctive Sardinian drink, mirto (see page 153) is made from myrtle, while Ichnusa beer is exported around the world. Mineral water is bottled from pure mountain springs all over the island, both commercially and by people out for a drive who bring along large bottles to refill, though none of it is currently exported.

Cheese is one of Sardinia's most basic foods, served at almost every meal. Sardinian shepherds have always preserved any leftover milk from their flocks by making cheese, and sheep's milk cheese – pecorino (see page 199) – is a distinctive part of Sardinia's cuisine. The leftover whey is re-cooked (*ri-cotta* in Italian) to make a delicious, fragile, sheep's milk ricotta (*recottu* in Sardinian dialect), which is sometimes also smoked. *Casu axedu* is a fresh curd made from sheep's or goat's milk soured with whey and drained overnight; it has a fresh, slightly acidic flavour. Drained for longer and preserved in brine it's called *fiscidu* or *frue*; similar to *ricotta salata* (salted ricotta) or feta, it originated around the provinces of Ogliastra and Nuoro, where it's added to potato and fregola soup and used in potato and mint ravioli (*culurzones*; see page 24).

Goat's milk cheeses, both fresh and aged, are also made, as is goat's milk ricotta from the whey. *Callu de cabreddu* (or *cabrettu*, depending on your dialect) is an ancient goat's milk cheese aged in the stomach of a young goat for about 4 months and smoked; it has a tangy flavour, strong aroma and creamy consistency.

Pear-shaped *casizzolu*, also called *peretta* because of its shape, is one of Sardinia's few cow's milk cheeses. This stretched-curd cheese (a type of *caciocavallo*) is made with milk from the Sardinian-Modican breed, red cows that graze the pastures of Montiferru in the province of Oristano. It's popular fried and served drizzled with honey.

See also
- Gallurese-style Bread Pudding (page 15) in 'Bread'
- Deep-fried Stuffed Zucchini Flowers (page 48) in 'Vegetables'
- Snapper with White Wine, Green Olives and Parsley (page 83) in 'Seafood'
- Fillet of Beef with Turnip Tops. Bottarga Butter and Red Wine Sauce (page 122) in 'Meat and Poultry'
- Hare Braised in Mirto (page 153) in 'Hunting and Foraging'
- Wild Boar Stew (page 154) in 'Hunting and Foraging'
- Trout with White Wine and Rosemary (page 158) in 'Hunting and Foraging'
- Nettle Tagliolini with Pecorino, Black Pepper and Cured Pork Cheek (page 162) in 'Hunting and Foraging'
- Cherries Poached in Mirto with Sheep's Milk Yoghurt Ice Cream (page 168) in 'Pastries and Desserts'
- Pears Poached in Red Wine with Ginger Semifreddo (page 190) in 'Pastries and Desserts'

RICOTTA AND PECORINO TARTS

CASADINAS

MAKES ABOUT 40

100 g sultanas
350 g well-drained ricotta (see page 221)
150 g young Pecorino Sardo, freshly grated
60 g fine semolina (see page 221), sifted
pinch fine sea salt
¼ teaspoon saffron threads
3 eggs, lightly beaten
100 g castor sugar
finely grated zest of 1 orange
finely grated zest of 1 lemon

CASADINAS DOUGH

400 g tipo oo flour, plus extra for dusting
pinch fine sea salt
2 egg whites, lightly beaten
about 1 cup (250 ml) water
25 g butter, melted

These free-form tarts are called *formagelle* in Italian and *pardulas* in another Sardinian dialect, but in my dialect they're *casadinas* and we traditionally make them for Easter. If you have a pasta machine, use it to roll the dough as thinly as possible; if you don't, use a rolling pin. This recipe makes quite a few: it can easily be halved, but the tarts will keep well for a week covered and refrigerated – just warm them through in a 100°C oven for 10 minutes or so before serving.

Cover sultanas with warm water and set aside for about 30 minutes to reconstitute; drain and pat dry.

To make the casadinas dough, sift flour and salt into the bowl of an electric mixer fitted with a dough hook. With the machine running, pour in the egg whites then 150 ml of the water and mix until absorbed. Mix in butter, then start adding remaining water, a little at a time, to form a firm dough; you may not need it all – towards the end it doesn't take much extra water for the dough to become too soft. Tip dough onto a clean, lightly floured workbench and knead with the heels of your hands for about 5 minutes, until smooth and elastic. Wrap in plastic wrap and set aside for about 1 hour.

Meanwhile, push ricotta through a fine sieve into a mixing bowl. Stir in pecorino, semolina, sultanas, salt and saffron. Add beaten egg, one third at a time, mixing well between additions. Stir in sugar, then lemon and orange zests, and mix well.

Cut the dough in half and, using a rolling pin on a clean, lightly floured workbench, flatten slightly. Cover one piece of dough with a clean tea towel to prevent it drying out. Pass the other piece through a pasta machine on the widest setting, then fold in half and pass again, then fold in half and pass a third time. Reduce the setting by a notch and pass the dough through the machine three more times, reducing the setting by a notch each time, dusting lightly with a little flour if it starts to stick. It should end up about 2 mm thick. Whenever the dough gets too long to handle, cut it in half and continue with each half separately, keeping any dough that isn't being rolled under the tea towel. Repeat with remaining dough.

Preheat oven to 150°C and line two baking trays with baking paper. Lay a sheet of pastry out on a clean, lightly floured workbench and cut out discs with a 9 cm round cutter. Place discs on a clean tea towel and cover with another clean tea towel. Cover leftover pastry with a clean tea towel as well. Repeat with remaining pastry, then re-roll off-cuts to make more discs.

Place a heaped teaspoon of filling in the centre of a disc and gently press it down to flatten a little. Fold the sides of the disc up, pinching them to form a cup around the filling. Using an egg lifter or fish slice, carefully place the filled tart on one of the prepared baking trays. Cover with a clean tea towel and repeat with remaining pastry discs and filling.

Place trays in oven and cook for 20 minutes, then swap the positions of the trays and cook for a further 20 minutes or so, until the filling is well browned. Remove from oven and set aside to cool. Serve just warm.

PECORINO

Pecorino, from *pecora* ('sheep'), is the generic name for Italy's pale sheep's milk cheeses, made since ancient times and usually named for their region of origin.

Pecorino is a staple of the Sardinian pantry, eaten at any time of day, and Sardinia is the only region to produce three pecorino cheeses with PDO appellation (Protected Designation of Origin): Pecorino Sardo, Fiore Sardo and Pecorino Romano.

Pecorino Sardo PDO is a semi-cooked cheese made from raw sheep's milk in 1.7–4 kg cylinders. Unusually for a sheep's milk cheese, it is set with calf's rennet. Pecorino Sardo is sold in two forms: matured for 20–60 days, it's sold as *dolce* ('young'); matured for between 2 and 12 months, it's sold as *maturo* ('aged'), which is occasionally also smoked. *Dolce* has a supple texture with mild, slightly tangy flavour, while the firmer *maturo* is nutty and slightly sweet until about 6 months of age; after that, it becomes more granular with a stronger flavour, and is mainly used for grating.

Pecorino Romano PDO is a cooked cheese made from raw sheep's milk that evolved around Rome (as the name suggests), but is now mostly made in Sardinia, where more land is available for sheep grazing. Made in 20–35 kg cylinders, it is larger than other pecorinos, and is set with lamb's rennet. It's aged for at least 5 months and is harder than Pecorino Sardo, with a stronger, more acidic flavour.

Sardinia's oldest-known cheese, Fiore Sardo PDO, pre-dates Roman times and is named for the vegetable extract that was traditionally used instead of rennet to set the curds (*fiore* means 'flower'), though lamb's or kid's rennet is used today. These thick, bulging wheels of uncooked cheese made from raw or pasteurised milk were traditionally made by shepherds in the mountainous Barbagia area of Nuoro and aged for 2–8 months in their huts, where the fires added a smoky character to the hard, nutty cheese.

Casu marzu (also called *casu frazigu*, both of which are dialect terms for 'rotten cheese'), is a Sardinian delicacy from Nuoro that is definitely an acquired taste. Pecorino, usually Fiore Sardo, is infested with cheese-fly larvae, which break the cheese down to a very soft consistency with a sharp, tangy flavour. You eat it with one hand shielding your eyes so the maggots don't jump into them. Not surprisingly, it's banned from sale, and can only be made for home consumption – but, in true Italian fashion, it's listed as a 'traditional food product' by the Italian government.

RICOTTA CAKE WITH WALNUTS, ALMONDS AND CANDIED ORANGE

TORTA DI RICOTTA CON NOCI, MANDORLE E ARANCE CANDITE

SERVES 8

100 g sultanas
70 g shelled walnuts
70 g blanched almonds
500 g ricotta
100 ml full-cream milk
3 eggs
250 g self-raising flour
300 g castor sugar
70 g candied orange, finely diced
butter, for greasing
plain flour, for dusting

This cake is delicious for afternoon tea. To serve it as a dessert, accompany it with mascarpone whipped with a few drop of vanilla extract and some finely grated lemon zest.

Cover sultanas with warm water and set aside for about 30 minutes to reconstitute; drain and pat dry. Place walnuts and most of the almonds (reserving 8 for decoration) in a blender and pulse until coarsely ground.

Place ricotta in a large bowl and, using a wooden spoon, beat in the milk until smooth. Beat in the eggs, one at time. Sift a third of the flour into the bowl and fold it into the ricotta mixture, sift in another third and fold in, then sift in the remaining third and fold in. Fold in the sugar. Fold sultanas into the mixture, then the candied orange, and finally the ground walnuts and almonds.

Preheat oven to 160°C.

Grease a 22 cm springform cake tin with butter and dust lightly with flour, shaking out any excess. Pour mixture into the tin and, using a spatula, spread it out evenly. Cut remaining almonds into quarters lengthways and scatter over the top of the mixture. Bake in oven for 1 hour and 10 minutes, then test by inserting a wooden skewer: if it comes out dry, the cake is ready; if there is mixture clinging to the skewer, return to the oven for a further 5 minutes then test again.

Remove from oven and leave in the tin to rest for 5 minutes, then turn out onto a wire rack to cool. Serve at room temperature.

Note
Candied orange is available from some delicatessens.

DEEP-FRIED CHEESE PASTRIES

SEADAS

SERVES 8 (MAKES BOUT 16)

50 g sultanas
500 g well-drained ricotta (see page 221)
1 egg yolk
100 g castor sugar
finely grated zest of 2 lemons
vegetable oil, for deep-frying
corbezzolo honey (see page 177)
   or other honey, for serving

SEADAS PASTRY

500 g plain flour, plus extra for dusting
pinch fine sea salt
200 ml warm water
50 g lard, at room temperature

This is _the_ classic Sardinian dessert, served all over the island. In some areas the pastries are filled with young pecorino instead of ricotta. Lard was traditionally used to make the pastry because that's what people had on hand. It gives a distinctive flaky texture and is still used by most people today; however, you can use butter, if you prefer. It's easier to make this pastry using a pasta machine to roll it out.

Cover sultanas with warm water and set aside for about 30 minutes to reconstitute; drain and pat dry.

Meanwhile, make the seadas pastry. Sift the flour and salt into the bowl of an electric mixer fitted with a dough hook. With the machine running, pour in the water and mix until it has a stretchy texture, then add the lard and mix in by hand to make a firm, smooth dough. Tip the dough onto a clean, lightly floured workbench and knead with the heels of your hands for about 5 minutes, until smooth and elastic. Roll into a ball, wrap in plastic wrap and refrigerate for about 30 minutes.

Push ricotta through a fine sieve. Using a balloon whisk, beat in the egg yolk, followed by the sugar, then the lemon zest (don't use an electric mixer, as this may overwork the mixture, causing the ricotta to split). Fold through the sultanas.

Cut the dough into two pieces and, using a rolling pin, flatten slightly. Pass each piece through a pasta machine on the widest setting, then fold in half and repeat, reducing the setting by a notch each time, until the pastry is about 2 mm thick.

Lay a sheet of pastry on a clean, lightly floured workbench. With a 10 cm round cutter, lightly mark out a row of discs along one side of the pastry; you'll need just over half the pastry to fold back over the filling. Place 2 tablespoons of ricotta mixture in the centre of each disc. Fold over the other half of the pastry to completely cover the filling, pressing gently around each mound of filling to eliminate as much air as possible. Use the 10 cm cutter to gently mark the dough around each mound of filling, then use a wheel pastry cutter to cut out the pastries. Place them on a lightly floured tray and repeat with remaining pastry and filling.

Heat vegetable oil to 160°C (if you don't have a deep-frying thermometer, test the temperature of the oil by dipping the handle of a wooden spoon into it – when bubbles form around the spoon, the oil is hot enough).

Meanwhile, place honey in a small saucepan over low heat and warm without boiling.

Lower pastries carefully into hot oil and deep-fry, a few at a time, for about 4 minutes, until underside is golden, then turn and fry other side for about 3 minutes, until golden. Drain on paper towel.

Serve drizzled with warm honey.

RICOTTA FRITTERS WITH HONEY

FRITTELLE DI RICOTTA CON MIELE

SERVES 8 (MAKES ABOUT 24)

35 g sultanas
500 g well-drained ricotta (see page 221)
3 egg yolks
100 g castor sugar
1 teaspoon vanilla extract
75 g plain flour
1 teaspoon baking powder
finely grated zest of 1 orange
finely grated zest of 1 lemon
50 g dark chocolate, coarsely grated
35 g pine nuts, toasted (see page 222)
vegetable oil, for deep-frying
1 cup (360 g) millefiori honey
   (see page 177) or other honey,
   for serving

These little fritters are crisp and dark on the outside and very soft on the inside. Serve them with a spoonful of mascarpone or a scoop of Sheep's Milk Yoghurt Ice Cream (see page 168), if you like.

Cover sultanas with warm water and set aside for about 30 minutes to reconstitute them; drain and pat dry.

Press ricotta through a fine sieve into a bowl. Using a wooden spoon, beat in egg yolks, sugar, and vanilla extract until smooth.

Sift flour and baking powder together, then sift over ricotta mixture in bowl and fold in. Fold in orange and lemon zests, chocolate, pine nuts and sultanas, then cover and refrigerate for about 1 hour.

Heat vegetable oil to 160°C (if you don't have a deep-frying thermometer, test the temperature of the oil by dipping the handle of a wooden spoon into it – when bubbles form around the spoon, the oil is hot enough).

Meanwhile, place honey in a small saucepan over low heat and warm gently, without boiling.

Form quenelles of the ricotta mixture by transferring spoonfuls of the mixture between two tablespoons, smoothing it as you go, to form egg shapes, then gently slide them into the hot oil. Deep-fry until underside is brown then turn and fry the other side.

Remove from oil, drain on paper towel and serve drizzled with warm honey.

QUINCE PASTE

CHIDONZADA

MAKES ABOUT 40 PIECES

2 lemons
9 quinces
2 oranges
100 ml red mirto (see page 153)
500 g–1 kg castor sugar, depending
   on size of quinces

Dried fruit pastes like this are popular all over the Middle East and this sweet, which I remember always being served on lemon leaves in Sardinia, is another example of the Arabic influence. You'll need muslin to wrap the quince cores in; if you don't have any, you can just put the cores in with the quinces, but they'll be harder to remove. A perfect partner for cheese, quince paste is also great served after a meal, with coffee or a dessert wine – in which case, you can sprinkle half the diamonds with hundreds and thousands.

Squeeze one of the lemons into a bowl of water, then drop the squeezed halves into the bowl.

Peel and core quinces, reserving cores. Cut quince into 3 cm pieces and place in the lemon water to prevent discolouration. Wrap quince cores in muslin and tie into a bag with kitchen string.

Wash oranges, then peel skin off in wide strips.

Place drained quinces, muslin bag with cores, orange peel, mirto, 300 ml of water and the juice of the remaining lemon in a saucepan. Bring to the boil, then reduce heat to medium and cook for about an hour until a wooden skewer can be inserted into the quince without any resistance. Drain, discarding quince cores and orange peel, then purée quince in a blender until smooth.

Weigh the quince purée, then measure out three-quarters of that weight in sugar. Place sugar and quince purée in a saucepan over low heat and cook for 3–4 hours, stirring often, until it becomes quite dark and is thick enough that a wooden spoon will stand up in it.

Line a 30 cm × 24 cm tray with baking paper, then spread the quince paste on this to a thickness of about 1.5 cm. Set aside to cool, then cover and refrigerate overnight.

Slice, on the diagonal, into 4 cm wide strips, then slice in the opposite direction, on the diagonal to form diamond shapes. Serve as a sweetmeat or with cheese.

GRAPE SYRUP AND SEMOLINA PASTE

LA MOSTARDA DI CARLOFORTE

MAKES 12 PIECES

200 ml saba (see page 221)
50 g coarse semolina (see page 221)

From left to right: Quince Paste (this page); Grape Syrup and Semolina Paste (this page); Sardinian Spiced Nut Bread (page 9)

***La mostarda** is served as an accompaniment to cheese; at the restaurant we use a saba flavoured with quince to make it, which adds a great taste.*

Line a tray with baking paper.

Bring saba to the boil in a medium-sized saucepan. Slowly 'rain' in the semolina, whisking constantly until well combined. Reduce heat to as low as possible and, stirring constantly with a wooden spoon, cook for 10 minutes.

Tip onto the prepared tray, cover with baking paper and roll out to a thickness of about 1 cm. Refrigerate for at least 2 hours, then cut into pieces about 3 cm square.

SARDINIAN WINES

Phoenicians were most likely the first to make wine from Sardinia's native grapes, and the Catalans later introduced a number of Spanish varietals to the island. But, less than 20 years ago, Sardinia was still lucky to be deemed worthy of more than a paragraph in a book on the wine regions of the world. It produced quaffable whites for the tourist crowds on the Costa Smeralda; heavy, often oxidative, reds, mainly from Cannonau, drunk by the locals; and bulk wine used to add weight to wines produced in other, cooler regions. Today that's changing, as Sardinia is hailed as one of the 'emerging wine regions' of Europe, with 1 wine with DOCG (*Denominazione di Origine Controllata e Garantita*) appellation, 19 with DOC (*Denominazione di Origine Controllata*) and 15 with IGT (*Indicazione Geographica Tipica*) status (including the generic Isola dei Nuraghi, which applies to the whole island), the most of any Italian region. Officially, Italy's DOCG and DOC appellations are now covered by the European Union's PDO (*Protected Denomination of Origin* – DOP in Italian), while IGT wines come under their PGI (*Protected Geographical Indication* – IGP in Italian) designation. In practice, however, Italy has been slow to adopt these new European designations.

WHITE WINES

Vermentino (called Rolle in southern France and also popular in Corsica, Liguria and Tuscany) originated in Spain and is Sardinia's most important white wine. It is produced throughout the island (**Vermentino di Sardegna DOC**), mainly on the coast, but the best is produced in the cool, hilly northeastern tip: **Vermentino di Gallura DOCG**, which in 1996 became Sardinia's first (and currently only) DOCG wine. Vermentino grapes produce complex wines in a range of styles, some with a rich peach-like butteriness, while others have citrus, melon, floral and herbal notes. All have a lively acidity, and most have a slight, pleasant bitterness, making it popular as an *aperitivo*, as well as with seafood and rice dishes.

Vernaccia is an indigenous Sardinian grape, unrelated to other Italian Vernaccias; the name is common throughout Italy as it comes from the Latin *vernaculus*, meaning 'indigenous'. **Vernaccia di Oristano DOC** is produced from grapes grown on the sandy soil on the mid-west coast of Sardinia and is often used for cooking seafood; the appellation also covers a sherry-style wine (see page 210).

Nuragus, Sardinia's most widely-planted grape, may have been introduced by the Phoenicians. It grows abundantly, especially in the south, where **Nuragus di Cagliari DOC** is a juicy, floral, easy-drinking wine, though most Nuragus ends up in blends.

Torbato is thought to be a Spanish variety. It was once widely planted in Rousillon in France, where it was called Tourbat, though it's now mostly associated with Sardinia. It's grown around Alghero in the northwest by Sella & Mosca and produces a creamy, slightly spicy wine.

Semidano, grown all over the island, is mostly used for blending, though it does have an appellation, **Sardegna Semidano DOC**, which covers dry and sweet, still and sparkling white wines.

RED WINES

Cannonau is Sardinia's most famous red wine. It was introduced by the Spaniards, who call it Garnacha (the French know it as Grenache, while in Tuscany it's Alicante). The appellation **Cannonau di Sardegna DOC** applies to the entire island, but the best is produced inland, in Nuoro, in the commune of Oliena. It produces deeply coloured, dry, earthy, medium- to full-bodied wines, often with a high alcohol content, that are good with meat ragùs, roasted meat (especially suckling pig), game and cheese. A rosé (*rosato*) is also made under the DOC appellation.

Carignano is also from Spain, where it's called Cariñena or Mazuelo (in southern France, it's known as Carignan). Almost exclusively planted in the southwest, including the islands of San Pietro and Sant'Antioco, the best wines produced from this variety are **Carignano del Sulcis DOC**. Earthy, full-bodied wines with a lingering aroma, they're great with roast lamb or mutton and goat dishes. A rosé is also made under the DOC appellation.

Monica, of Spanish origin and grown throughout the island, is sold under the appellation **Monica di Sardegna DOC**, but the best, **Monica di Cagliari DOC**, comes from the rolling Campidano plains in the south. It's a dry, medium-bodied, savoury wine with an intense aroma.

Bovale, introduced from Spain, has two distinct varieties: **Bovale Sardo** (also called Bovaleddu, Muristellu/Muristella, Manca dell'Arca or Bovali Piticcu), which is found throughout the island and sometimes used to produce single varietal wines; and **Bovale di Spagna** (or Bovali Mannu), which is most common in Oristano province and mostly used in blends. Experts disagree as to whether **Nièddera** is a separate grape variety or a regional name for Bovale di Spagna.

Girò was probably introduced from Spain; **Girò di Cagliari DOC** covers both dry and sweet still wines produced in the south and southwest.

Pascale di Cagliari (despite its name) and **Cagnulari** grow mainly around Sassari (in the north) and are usually blended with other reds such as Cannonau.

SWEET AND FORTIFIED WINES AND DISTILLATES

Passitu (the Sardinian name for Italian *passito*) wines made from dried grapes are common in Sardinia's hot, dry climate, as are other sweet wines, whether they're late-harvest or fortified. Some sparkling wines are also made.

Vernaccia di Oristano DOC in its sweet form tastes similar to dry amontillado sherry and has some similarities in its production. It's aged in chestnut barrels under a layer of flor, sometimes in a solera-style system, sometimes as a single vintage; it differs from sherry, however, in that it's rarely fortified. Released at around 2 years it's popular served with bottarga; aged to at least 4 years (*riserva*), it's served as an *aperitivo*, as well as with creamy pasta and desserts. The appellation also covers a dry table wine (see page 209).

Moscato di Sardegna DOC is a sweet sparkling wine produced all over the island from Muscat grapes. **Moscato di Cagliari DOC** is a sweet, slightly sparkling wine from the south and southwest. **Moscato di Sorso-Sennori DOC** applies to two still white wines, one naturally sweet and one fortified; both are made from Moscato Bianco grown in a small area on the north coast near Sassari.

Malvasia di Cagliari DOC covers dry, sweet and fortified white wines made from Malvasia Sarda, which has a distinctive bitter-almond finish. The **Malvasia di Bosa DOC** appellation, which also covers dry, sweet and fortified white wines made from Malvasia, applies to wines made in the Planargia hills on the mid-west coast, though perhaps from a different clone to that growing around Cagliari.

Nasco di Cagliari DOC, applies to dry still or sparkling white wines and sweet still white wine made from Nasco, a grape native to the south and southwest of Sardinia. Sweet late harvest or *passitu* wines are most common.

Cannonau is used to make two sweet red wines under its DOC appellation: *liquoroso dolce* has a minimum alcohol of 16 per cent, and *liquoroso secco*, 18 per cent.

Filu 'e Ferru is the Sardinian name for grappa, distilled from the must leftover after the grapes are pressed to make wine. The name is dialect for 'wire thread', because in the days of illegal stills the bottles of grappa were buried and the spot marked with a thin piece of wire tied to the neck of the bottle and protruding from the ground.

OTHER SARDINIAN DOC APPELLATIONS

Alghero DOC applies to red, white and rosé wines produced on the plains between Alghero and Sassari.

Arborea DOC was created in the late 1980s to encourage red, white and rosé wines made with Sangiovese and Trebbiano grown on the alluvial plains around Oristano, but very few such wines are produced.

Campidano di Terralba DOC is a light dry red from the plains south of Oristano which contains, among other grapes, both Bovale Sardo and Bovale di Spagna.

Mandrolisai DOC covers red and rosé wines produced on the rocky soil of the Barbagia hills, a small area in central Sardinia, from a variety of grapes including Cannonau, Monica and Bovale Sardo.

TASTING SUGGESTIONS

As Sardinia gains recognition as an emerging wine region, the range and availability of the island's wines is getting better all the time. If you're keen to try some Sardinian wines for yourself, look for the following:

Argiolas

Originally established in 1938 in the province of Cagliari to produce bulk wines for other wineries, this producer has been bottling their own wines since 1990 – mainly Vermentino, Nuragus, Monica and Cannonau – with leading oenologist Giacomo Tachis acting as their consultant. Their premium wine, Turriga, a barrique-aged blend of mainly Cannonau and Carignano, and the partially barrique-aged white Angialis, an IGT *passitu* made from Nasco and Malvasia, are two of Sardinia's benchmark wines. They also produce good Vermentino di Sardegna DOC and Cannonau di Sardegna DOC.

Cantina Gallura

Located at Tempio Pausania, this is one of the best cooperatives: try their Karana, an IGT wine made primarily from Nebbiolo, and their range of Vermentino di Gallura DOCG.

Cantina di Santadi

Established in 1960, this cooperative is in the Sulcis area of Cagliari, one of the few phylloxera-free areas of Europe. With one of Italy's top oenologists, Giacomo Tachis, as a consultant, they have a strong focus on quality. Internationally recognised, their Carignano del Sulcis DOC is made in several styles, including the juicy Rocca Rubia, barrique-aged for 10–12 months, and the heavier Terre Brune, barrique-aged for 18-20 months. Latinia is their dessert wine, made from late-harvest Nasco grapes.

Capichera

Established in the 19th century in Arzachena, near Olbia, this is now Gallura's most highly regarded estate. In the 1970s they undertook new plantings and built new facilities, so they could begin bottling their own wines with an emphasis on low yields and best practice at every stage of the process, including organic farming. They've produced wine under the Capichera label since 1980, and in 1990 produced the late-harvest Vendemmia Tardiva (VT), the first Vermentino fermented and entirely aged in barriques. Their second label, Kharisma, is also worth looking out for.

Azienda Vinicola Contini

Established in 1898, this is one of Sardinia's oldest family-owned wineries and the leading producer of Vernaccia di Oristano DOC, which they make in various styles, including a *riserva* with a complex nuttiness and Antico Gregori, which is aged in a solera-style system. They also produce Vermentino, Cannonau and Nièddera, including a rosé.

Tenute Dettori

This small (33-hectare) family-run estate in Sennori, near Sassari, produces handcrafted wines with minimal intervention. They grow Cannonau, Monica, Pascale, Vermentino and Moscato grapes, and their wines, all single varietals, are rather esoteric in style.

Pala

Based in Serdiana, a small town just outside Cagliari, this producer was established in 1950 to produce bulk wines for other wineries. In the hands of the founder's son since 1995, it has become a modern winery with a focus on quality, producing Vermentino, Cannonau, Monica, Bovale, Nuragus, Nasco and Malvasia, which are used in single varietals and blends.

BASIC RECIPES

STOCKS

Often traditional recipes didn't use stock; just water; if there was no animal for the pot, then there weren't any meat scraps for the stockpot. If you're making stock, it's generally worth making a large quantity so you always have some in the freezer. Freeze it in plastic containers for up to 6 months. If your stockpot isn't large enough, however, just halve the recipe.

When straining stocks it's important to ladle the liquid through a lined sieve, rather than pouring it directly from the pan. Otherwise you'll stir up the sediment and make the stock go cloudy – and you should always discard the last few centimetres of stock at the bottom the pot, as it will be laden with sediment.

FISH STOCK
BRODO DI PESCE

MAKES ABOUT 2 LITRES

1 kg white fish bones and heads
3 slices lemon
1 brown onion, peeled and quartered
1 small carrot, halved
1 bay leaf
a few black peppercorns
3 stalks flat-leaf parsley
½ cup (125 ml) Vermentino (see page 219) or other dry white wine

Fish bones and heads are available from most fishmongers. It's important to use only bones from white, non-oily fish (snapper is ideal), as bones from oily fish such as salmon will make a very strong-tasting stock.

Place all ingredients in a stockpot or large saucepan and just cover with cold water.

Bring to the boil, then reduce heat and simmer for 15–20 minutes, skimming regularly to remove any froth that rises to the surface (this will help prevent the stock from going cloudy).

Set aside to cool, then ladle through a sieve lined with muslin or a clean damp Chux or J-Cloth, discarding solids.

PRAWN STOCK
BRODO DI GAMBERI

MAKES ABOUT 2.5 LITRES

500 g prawn heads and shells
1 bulb baby fennel, halved
1 stalk celery
4 roma (plum) tomatoes
1 brown onion
¼ cup (60 ml) olive oil
½ bunch flat-leaf parsley, torn
½ bunch dill, torn
100 ml Cinzano bianco
2 bay leaves
10 white peppercorns
3 litres water

Whenever you peel prawns for a dish, save the heads and shells and freeze them until you have enough to make this stock.

Wash prawn shells and heads, and fennel, well in cold water. Roughly chop fennel, celery, tomatoes and onion.

Heat a stockpot or large saucepan over high heat, add oil and, when hot, add prawn heads and shells and cook for 3–5 minutes until coloured. Add Cinzano and cook for a minute or two until it starts to boil.

Add remaining ingredients and return to the boil. Reduce heat and simmer for 1 hour, skimming regularly to remove any froth that rises to the surface (this will help prevent the stock from going cloudy).

Set aside to cool, then ladle through a sieve lined with muslin or a clean damp Chux or J-Cloth, discarding solids.

CHICKEN STOCK
BRODO DI POLLO

MAKES ABOUT 5 LITRES

4 raw chicken carcasses
1 leek, roughly chopped
2 carrots, roughly chopped
2 stalks celery, roughly chopped
4 small brown onions, roughly chopped
1 bunch flat-leaf parsley, torn
3 bay leaves
2 sprigs rosemary
1 head garlic, halved horizontally
1 tablespoon white peppercorns
8 litres cold water

Chicken stock has the most neutral flavour of any stock and so is used as a base in many dishes, including risotto and some seafood dishes. It's worth always keeping some in the freezer.

Wash the carcasses and leek in cold water. Place leek, carrots, celery and onions in a stockpot or large saucepan. Pack in the chicken carcasses, halving them if necessary. Add remaining ingredients and bring to the boil.

Reduce heat and simmer for 6 hours, skimming regularly to remove any froth that rises to the surface (this will help prevent the stock from going cloudy).

Set aside to cool, then ladle through a sieve lined with muslin or a clean damp Chux or J-Cloth, discarding solids.

VEAL STOCK
BRODO DI VITELLO

MAKES ABOUT 4 LITRES

2 kg veal bones, chopped
  (ask your butcher to do this)
3 carrots, roughly chopped
1 large brown onion, roughly chopped
2 stalks celery, roughly chopped
6 bay leaves
1 bunch flat-leaf parsley, torn
20 black peppercorns
½ teaspoon salt flakes

This stock takes a long time to cook, so it's worth making as big a batch as your stockpot will allow and freezing some for later use.

Place bones in a stockpot or large saucepan, cover with water and bring to the boil, then strain and rinse well.

Return veal bones to a clean stockpot or large saucepan and cover with about 6 litres of fresh cold water – the bones should be completely submerged – then bring to the boil.

Reduce heat, skim off any froth that rises to the surface, then add remaining ingredients and simmer for 6–8 hours, skimming regularly (this will help prevent the stock from going cloudy). If the liquid level drops so that the ingredients are uncovered, top up with a little cold water.

Set aside to cool, then ladle through a sieve lined with muslin or a clean damp Chux or J-Cloth, discarding solids.

MUTTON STOCK

BRODO DI PECORA

MAKES ABOUT 4 LITRES

2 kg mutton bones, chopped
   (ask your butcher to do this)
3 carrots, roughly chopped
1 large brown onion, roughly chopped
2 stalks celery, roughly chopped
6 roma (plum) tomatoes, quartered
1 tablespoon tomato paste (purée)
6 bay leaves
1 bunch flat-leaf parsley, torn
20 black peppercorns
½ teaspoon salt flakes

Mutton stock is distinctly Sardinian; it's normally the cooking liquid left over from making Boiled Mutton (see page 120). As this stock is quite strong, it's only used in certain dishes, such as Gallurese-style Bread Pudding (see page 15).

Place bones in a stockpot or large saucepan, cover with water and bring to the boil, then strain and rinse well.

Return mutton bones to a clean stockpot or large saucepan, cover with about 6 litres of fresh cold water – the bones should be completely submerged – then bring to the boil.

Reduce heat, skim off any froth that rises to the surface, then add remaining ingredients and simmer for 6–8 hours, skimming regularly (this will help prevent the stock from going cloudy). If the liquid level drops so that the ingredients are uncovered, top up with a little cold water.

Set aside to cool, then ladle through a sieve lined with muslin or a clean damp Chux or J-Cloth, discarding solids.

VEGETABLE STOCK

BRODO DI VERDURE

MAKES ABOUT 5 LITRES

1 brown onion, roughly chopped
1 stalk celery, roughly chopped
1 carrot, roughly chopped
¼ leek, roughly chopped
handful flat-leaf parsley stalks
¼ bunch thyme
2 sprigs rosemary
5 g dried porcini (optional)
3 roma (plum) tomatoes, quartered
6 bay leaves
20 black peppercorns
salt flakes, to taste
5 litres water

Vegetable stock is usually made from whatever vegetable trimmings happen to be on hand. Dried porcini are available from some delicatessens and specialty food stores, but you could use mushroom stalks and trimmings instead or just leave them out.

Place all ingredients in a stockpot or large saucepan, and bring to the boil.

Reduce heat to low, skim off any froth that rises to the surface and simmer for 1 hour, skimming regularly (this will help prevent the stock from going cloudy).

Set aside to cool, then ladle through a sieve lined with muslin or a clean damp Chux or J-Cloth, discarding solids.

FRESH PASTA

Making fresh pasta is easy if you have a pasta machine – you just need to follow the steps of passing the dough through the machine on various settings to stretch it, then folding and passing it through again until you achieve the silky texture that makes this type of pasta so special. Different brands of machines use different numbering systems: some start at 10 for the widest setting and work down; others start at 0 and work up. These recipes can be successfully halved, but don't try making less than 300 g of pasta dough. Fresh pasta can always be frozen: dust with flour, spread it out on a tray and put the tray in the freezer for 6–8 hours, or overnight, until frozen. Remove the pasta and place in a freezer bag, extracting as much air as possible, then tie tightly and freeze for up to 6 months.

Rolling pasta dough

If using a pasta machine, cut dough into 4 pieces and flatten 1 piece slightly, wrapping remaining pieces in plastic wrap to prevent them drying out.

Pass the flattened piece of dough through a pasta machine on the widest setting, then fold it in half. Repeat the passing and folding three more times.

Reduce the setting on the machine a notch and pass the dough through, then pass two more times, reducing the setting each time and dusting the dough lightly with flour if it starts to stick.

Turn the setting back up to the widest one, fold pasta sheet in thirds (like a brochure) and pass through again. Pass the sheet through twice more, reducing the setting each time.

Fold pasta sheet in thirds again and rotate 90 degrees, then turn the setting on the machine back to the widest one and pass through. Keep passing the pasta sheet through multiple times, reducing the setting each time, until it is the required thickness for the specific pasta you're making (see details in individual recipes).

When the dough starts to get too long to handle, cut it in half, lightly dust the half you aren't working on with flour and continue with each half separately. If it becomes too long to handle again, cut in half again.

Repeat with remaining dough.

Cutting long pasta

Once you've made thin sheets of pasta by rolling the dough through the machine, you can make all sorts of pasta shapes using various attachments.

To make long pasta such as tagliolini and tonnarelli:

Lay a pasta sheet flat across the back of the machine with the end pointing into the teeth of the attachment, gently feed the end of the sheet into the teeth while slowly turning the handle.

Once the machine takes the sheet, place your hand gently on the sheet to keep it slightly taut while turning the handle – the machine will straighten the sheet up and take it through at the correct angle.

Once almost all of the sheet has passed through, change hands. Gather the strands of pasta together in one hand and turn the handle with the other hand to feed the remainder of the sheet through.

You'll be left holding a handful of beautiful fresh pasta strands. Place them on a flour-dusted tray and start again with the next pasta sheet.

With a little practice, you'll be whipping up trays of fresh pasta in no time at all.

FRESH PASTA DOUGH #1

MAKES ABOUT 800 G

500 g tipo oo flour, plus extra
   for dusting
2½ tablespoons fine sea salt
8 egg yolks
2 eggs

Variation

To make lemon pasta, add the finely
grated zest of 3 lemons to the eggs
before mixing them into the flour.

This dough is used for long pasta and shapes such as stracci (which literally means 'rags') – delicate pastas that are generally served with lighter sauces.

Sift flour and salt into the bowl of an electric mixer fitted with a dough hook. Lightly whisk egg yolks and eggs together, then with the machine running slowly drizzle most of the egg mixture into the flour and mix until absorbed.

Start adding the remaining egg a little at a time until you have a firm dough – you may not need it all; towards the end it doesn't take much extra liquid for the dough to become too soft.

Tip the dough onto a clean, lightly floured workbench and knead with the heels of your hands for about 5 minutes, until smooth and elastic. Roll into a ball, wrap in plastic wrap and refrigerate for about 1 hour.

FRESH PASTA DOUGH #2

MAKES ABOUT 850 G

500 g tipo oo flour, plus extra
   for dusting
2 teaspoons fine sea salt
11 egg yolks
2 eggs

Stuffed pasta requires a slightly softer dough than long pasta, so this dough has a couple of extra egg yolks added; if you halve this recipe, you'll have to weigh the egg yolks – you'll need 110 g.

Sift flour and salt into the bowl of an electric mixer fitted with a dough hook. Lightly whisk egg yolks and eggs together, then with the machine running slowly drizzle most of the egg mixture into the flour and mix until absorbed.

Start adding the remaining egg a little at a time until you have a firm dough – you may not need it all; towards the end it doesn't take much extra liquid for the dough to become too soft.

Tip the dough onto a clean, lightly floured workbench and knead with the heels of your hands for about 5 minutes, until smooth and elastic. Roll into a ball, wrap in plastic wrap and refrigerate for about 1 hour.

FRESH PASTA DOUGH #3

MAKES ABOUT 600 G

360 g semolina flour (see page 220),
   plus extra for dusting
pinch fine sea salt
about 200 ml warm water

Variations

For saffron pasta, soak 5 saffron threads
in ¼ cup (60 ml) of the water for a few
minutes and add it with the first lot of water.

For black pasta, whisk 2 teaspoons of
cuttlefish ink (available from delicatessens
and fishmongers) into the water.

For nettle pasta, reduce the amount of
water by 100 ml and mix 50 ml of nettle
purée (see page 162) into the water.

Pasta served with meat sauces is generally made from a dough that doesn't contain eggs. It is, however, often flavoured with saffron or cuttlefish ink – and this recipe also works well with other flavourings, including nettles. The recipe can be halved successfully, but if a recipe calls for less than 300 g of pasta dough, don't try making a smaller quantity; just freeze any excess dough and then thaw it in the fridge overnight before using.

Sift flour and salt into the bowl of an electric mixer fitted with a dough hook. With the machine running, pour in half the water and mix until absorbed.

Start adding the remaining water a little at a time until you have a firm dough – you may not need it all; towards the end it doesn't take much extra water for the dough to become too soft.

Tip the dough onto a clean, lightly floured workbench and knead with the heels of your hands for about 5 minutes, until smooth and elastic. Roll into a ball, wrap in plastic wrap and refrigerate for about 1 hour.

PASSATA

MAKES ABOUT 2 LITRES

⅓ cup (80 ml) extra virgin olive oil
1 brown onion, finely diced
3 cloves garlic, finely diced
4 kg very ripe tomatoes, washed
    and chopped
½ bunch basil, leaves picked and torn
salt flakes and freshly ground black
    pepper, to taste

This fresh tomato sauce is the base for so many dishes. The name passata refers to the fact that the tomatoes are 'passed' through a sieve to make a smooth sauce. When tomatoes are at their peak towards the end of summer, families spend weekends making passata and bottling it, so they will have a taste of summer through the colder months when tomatoes either aren't available or aren't at their best. I usually use roma (plum) tomatoes to make passata, as I find they have the most juice and flavour, but use whatever's abundant and really ripe and juicy. If you need passata for a recipe in winter, when tomatoes aren't ripe, and you don't have any stocks put aside, use Italian canned tomatoes.

Heat a saucepan over low–medium heat, add oil and, when hot, add onion and garlic and cook until soft but not coloured.

Add tomato, basil, salt and pepper and bring to the boil, then reduce heat and simmer for 1–1½ hours, stirring occasionally, until tomato has completely broken down into a thick sauce. If it dries out so much that it starts to stick, add a couple of tablespoons of water to loosen it up.

Pass the tomato sauce through a mouli, discarding skins and seeds. Store covered and refrigerated for a couple of days, or pack into sterilised jars and store in a cool, dark place for several months.

Note

If you don't have a mouli, it's much harder to make passata, but you could pass it through a sieve, pressing down with a ladle to extract as much liquid as possible. (Do not use a blender or food processor as it will pulverise the tomato seeds and spoil the flavour and colour.)

CHILLI MAYONNAISE
MAIONESE AL PEPERONCINO

MAKES ABOUT 1¼ CUPS (375 G)

2 egg yolks
1 teaspoon Dijon mustard
½ teaspoon white balsamic condiment
    (see page 221)
1 cup (250 ml) vegetable oil
salt flakes and freshly ground white
    pepper, to taste

CHILLI PASTE

½ long red chilli
2 small red chillies
50 ml vegetable oil

This mayonnaise is great with any fried food, and is also delicious on *panini* with tuna and tomato. Covered in the fridge, it will keep for up to a week.

For the chilli paste, preheat a char-grill or barbecue plate. Toss long chilli and small chillies in a little of the oil, then grill over a high heat for about 4 minutes, turning until well singed on all sides. Discard the stalk-ends, place chillies in a blender with remaining oil and process to form a smooth paste.

Place egg yolks, mustard and white balsamic in a bowl and whisk to combine.

Whisking constantly, slowly drizzle in the oil, a drop at a time to start with and then in a thin, steady stream. Whisk until all oil is incorporated and you have a thick mayonnaise.

Season with salt and pepper, then stir chilli paste into mayonnaise.

INGREDIENTS, EQUIPMENT AND COOKING TIPS

In a kitchen you have three things: your hands (that is, your skill), your ingredients and your equipment. If any of these aren't good, you can't produce good food. Most chefs are in love with equipment like great knives, copper pans and expensive machines; you don't need to spend a fortune on these, but you should buy the best equipment and the best ingredients you can afford. Skimping on the quality of your equipment or ingredients will show in the end product. As for skill, practice makes perfect!

SARDINIAN INGREDIENTS

Sardinia has a number of distinctive ingredients that add an authentic flavour to its cooking, and it's worth seeking them out in order to produce real Sardinian dishes. Many are now available through delicatessens; some are also available online, which is particularly helpful for cooks who don't live close to a major city (see the list of suppliers below for more details). Here are some of the Sardinian ingredients used in this book:

abbamele is made by boiling whole honeycomb with citrus zest and juice or water; if unavailable, you can make your own (see page 171) or simply use honey (see page 177).

Bosane olives are large green olives from Bosa, a small town on the west coast of Sardinia; if unavailable, use Sicilian green olives.

bottarga, dried grey mullet roe, adds a distinctive salty flavour to many Sardinian dishes (see page 93). It is encased in a thin membrane. If slicing bottarga, peel it first; if grating it, leave the membrane on to help hold the piece together – some of it will flake away as you grate and can easily be discarded; sift the grated bottarga to remove the rest.

Cannonau is Sardinia's most famous red wine (see page 209); if unavailable, use any dry, full-bodied red wine.

fregola is a toasted semolina pasta, similar to large couscous (see page 106). Some are handmade and others are machine-made, so the size can vary a little, and cooking times range from 7 to 10 minutes – it's best to follow the cooking instructions on the packet.

mirto is a bittersweet liqueur made from myrtle (see page 153).

pane carasau is Sardinian flatbread (see page 6), also called *carta di musica* or, in the dialect of my region, *pane fresa*.

Pecorino Sardo is Sardinian sheep's milk cheese (see page 199); if unavailable, use another Italian pecorino.

Vermentino is Sardinia's most common white wine (see page 209); if unavailable use any dry white wine.

Vernaccia di Oristano is a white wine made from an indigenous Sardinian grape (see page 209); if unavailable, use another dry white wine.

SUPPLIERS

Sardinian ingredients are becoming increasingly available, and there are a number of companies that sell online, making it possible to have a true taste of Sardinia, no matter where you live. Here are a few of the main ones:

Vallebona Sardinian Gourmet 020 8944 5665 www.vallebona.co.uk (an extensive range of Sardinian ingredients including cheeses, Sardinian-style *salumi*, bottarga and storecupboard items such as fregola and Sardinian olive oil).

Nife is Life 020 8961 0210 www.nifeislife.com (a good selection of Italian delicatessen items including Pecorina Sardo, fregola and Sardinian wines).

Palmavera: Sardinian fine foods 020 8360 3383 www.palmaverafinefoods.com (oils, *salame*, cheese, bottarga, pasta, *pane carasau*, Corbezzolo honey and *torrone*).

Melbury & Appleton 0843 2891880 www.melburyandappleton.co.uk (a selection of fine foods and drinks, including *saba*, Pecorino Sardo, bottarga and white balsamic condiment).

La Fromagerie 020 7359 7440 www.lafromagerie.co.uk (an extensive range of cheeses).

Good meat lifts a dish from good to great. Always source your meat locally where possible, but try good delicatessens online and butchers for the harder-to-find meats such as suckling pig, goat and offal.

OTHER INGREDIENTS

butter Use salted butter, unless a recipe specifies unsalted.

carnaroli rice is a medium-grained Italian rice that's ideal for risotto; it absorbs more liquid and holds its shape better than arborio rice and is larger, giving a better texture. The best brand is Acquerello, which is aged for up to 7 years.

celery Use the tender celery from the centre of the bunch (the heart); save the coarse outer stalks for making stock.

Cinzano bianco is an Italian white vermouth; if unavailable, use another white vermouth such as Noilly Prat.

dried Greek oregano is sold in delicatessens as whole stems with leaves and flower heads attached and is similar to the wild oregano that grows in Sardinia. To use it, crumble it between the palms of your hands and discard the stems. If it's unavailable, use regular dried oregano, but the aroma and flavour won't be as strong.

eggs for pasta dough and baking, where the exact amount of egg is important, use 67 g eggs, unless otherwise stated.

fennel I almost always use baby fennel because it's sweeter, more tender, and more like the wild fennel that grows in Sardinia. To prepare it, cut off the base and stems, keeping the fronds as they're great for garnish. Halve the bulb, discard any blemished outer layers, cut a 'v' in the base to remove the hard core, wash well as there's often some grit between the layers, then prepare according to the recipe. If baby fennel isn't available, use larger fennel, discarding more of the outer layers until you come to the tender centre.

flours Different kinds of flour are best suited to different purposes – using the right sort will ensure good results.

> **bread flour** Also called baker's flour or strong flour, this is made from hard wheat with a higher gluten content than regular flour – this gives it more elasticity, making it ideal for bread and other products that need to rise.

> **semolina flour** Made from durum wheat (the hardest variety of wheat), this flour is used for making dried pasta. It is not as fine as tipo oo flour, but is still flour and should not be confused with the granular product sold as 'semolina' or 'fine semolina' (see opposite).

> **tipo oo flour** Sometimes called *doppio zero* ('double zero'), this is flour that has been milled as finely as possible from soft wheat. It has a lower gluten content and can absorb more moisture than hard wheat flour, making it ideal for pastries and handmade pasta. If unavailable, use plain flour.

fruit and vegetables These are medium-sized unless otherwise stated.

guanciale is cured pork cheek; if unavailable, use pancetta, which is cured pork belly.

Italian sausages Buy any good Italian-style raw (uncured) pork sausages without added flavourings.

lard is rendered pork fat, and is available from supermarkets.

lardo, cured pork fat, is available from some delicatessens.

micro-herbs Micro- or baby herbs and cress, growing in punnets, are available at some greengrocers and online. They add both colour and flavour to dishes. Snip as many leaves as you need into a bowl of cold water – the herbs will float, and any soil or debris will sink – then skim off the herbs and drain on a clean tea towel. The remainder of the punnet will keep, loosely covered with a damp cloth and refrigerated, for several days; if micro-herbs are unavailable, use the smallest leaves on a bunch of the regular-sized herb or tear larger leaves into small pieces.

mint Use round-leaf mint (sometimes called Moroccan mint) for the recipes in this book. This is the common mint of Sardinia.

olive oil At home and in the restaurant I use extra virgin olive oil for everything, but different types for different purposes (see page 60 for information on Sardinian olive oil). A less-expensive oil, available in a large tin from supermarkets or delicatessens, is fine for cooking, but for finishing dishes, dressing salads or in sauces that rely heavily on the oil for flavour (such as a classic *aglio e olio* or the tagliolini with sea urchin on page 26), use the best-quality oil you can afford. For deep-frying, use vegetable oil.

potatoes There are many different types of potatoes available. To keep it simple I've used just three widely available types, and have given alternatives below; if these aren't available, ask your greengrocer for a suitable substitute.

> **desiree potatoes** These are good all-purpose potatoes that I use when I want a potato that mashes well; if unavailable, use nicola or king edward.

> **kipfler potatoes** These waxy potatoes don't fall apart when cooked; if unavailable, use pink fir.

> **spunta potatoes** These firm potatoes hold together well when cooked, but aren't as waxy as kipfler; if unavailable, use dutch cream.

ricotta, well-drained You need quite dry ricotta for some of the dishes in this book. If you buy ricotta that's very fresh and still quite moist, hang it in a clean damp Chux, J-Cloth or piece of muslin (as in the photo on page 194) over a bowl for a couple of hours in the fridge to firm it up; you'll lose about 25 per cent in liquid, so buy a bit more ricotta than you need.

saba, sometimes spelled *sapa*, is a syrup made from cooked grape must. It is known by various regional names throughout Italy, including *vin cotto* (literally 'cooked wine') and *mosto cotto* ('cooked must'). It's sometimes flavoured with other fruit, such as quince.

salt Fine sea salt is best for use in pastries and pasta water as it mixes in evenly and dissolves quickly. In Sardinia, people still harvest salt from Le Saline (near Olbia), a town named for the ancient salt flats there; they rake it up and take it home to use for salting their prosciutto and pancetta. It's also harvested commercially from the Molentargius wetlands near Cagliari. Use any good fine sea salt. Salt flakes are perfect in salads or for sprinkling over a finished dish.

semolina The product generally sold as 'semolina' is finely cracked durum wheat, at the stage before it is milled into flour; it is available in both coarse and fine versions. Do not confuse it with semolina flour (also called durum wheat flour – see opposite).

tomatoes There are many different size, shape and colour tomatoes available today. Sometimes I prefer a particular tomato for a dish because of the colour or shape, but if it doesn't taste good on the day, I'll always use another type – what matters most is always the flavour.

> **grape tomatoes** These are available in different colours, they look great halved and can be sweet and juicy; if they're unavailable, or are not great-tasting on the day, substitute cherry or teardrop tomatoes.

> **roma tomatoes** (also called plum tomatoes) This variety is my favourite tomato for making sauces; if I can't get good ones, I use truss cherry tomatoes. If fresh tomatoes are out of season, use drained canned Italian tomatoes; they have better flavour than anaemic unripe tomatoes or ones that have been gassed to make them look ripe.

> **truss cherry tomatoes** These are great for oven-roasting and presenting with the truss still attached.

> **vine-ripened tomatoes** These are best for salads.

Treviso radicchio This originated near the town of Treviso in Veneto, and is more readily available in winter. With long leaves, Treviso radicchio is shaped more like a cos lettuce than the common round radicchio – which is called Chioggia radicchio (after the town where it originated), and can be substituted for Treviso radicchio.

vongole (clams) Even if vongole have been purged when you buy them, toss them through a bowl of cold water with a tablespoon of plain flour and set aside for about 20 minutes; the flour irritates them and makes them spit out any remaining sand or grit.

white balsamic condiment is similar to a mild white wine vinegar, and is available from some delicatessens.

yeast, fresh Most bakers will be happy to sell you a small block of fresh yeast; it will keep, wrapped, in the fridge for up to a week or frozen for 3 months. When baking bread, the amount of yeast needed will vary depending on the temperature: the quantities in these recipes are suitable for most of the year, but in winter the yeast will work more slowly, so you'll need to use up to 25 per cent more. It's best to weigh yeast accurately, but if your scales aren't sensitive enough, 5 g is about 1 teaspoon.

zucchini flower, female Zucchini flowers can be either female, with an immature zucchini attached to the flower, or male, with just a thin stem attached; female flowers are best to use for the recipes in this book.

Ingredient substitutions and terms:

blue swimmer crab – can use langoustines.

kipfler potatoes – can use charlotte potatoes or any other waxy potatoes.

rocklobster – can use small lobsters or large langoustines.

scorpionfish – can use rock cod or any firm white fish.

spunta potatoes – can use charlotte potatoes or any other waxy potatoes.

trevela – can use cod.

witlof – also known as chicory.

COOKING TIPS

Apart from ingredients and equipment, the difference between a restaurant meal and one you prepare at home is often a number of small details in the preparation. Of course at the restaurant, I have a brigade of chefs and apprentices to help me, but you'll be surprised the difference it makes to your finished dish if you take a bit of extra time to get the details right.

cooking pasta Bring a large saucepan of water to the boil (you'll need at least 5 litres of water for 500 g pasta), then stir in 2 teaspoons fine sea salt per litre of water before adding the pasta (the water should taste salty, like the sea). When you drain the pasta, reserve some of the cooking liquid to add to the sauce: in an oil-based sauce this creates a creamy emulsion; a wet sauce (such as a *ragù* or *sugo*) may not need it, but keep a little aside just in case it is too dry. Add pasta to the sauce and toss it in the pan ten times. The tossing helps the starch from the pasta combine with the sauce, which is called *mantecare* in Italian. If mixing it in a saucepan, stir it at least ten times.

covering with foil When covering a baking dish with foil, it's important that the foil seals the dish really well; this is easiest to achieve if the dish has a slight lip. Run a cloth around the edge, pinching the foil firmly against the lip or side of the dish (if you do this without the cloth, the foil is likely to tear).

deep-frying It's important to deep-fry at the correct temperature: if the temperature's too low, the food will absorb too much oil and become greasy and soggy; and if it's too high; the outside will burn before the inside is cooked. Ideally, use a cooking thermometer to ensure the oil reaches the specified temperature before adding food to it, then be careful not to add too much food at one time, so the oil returns to this temperature as quickly as possible – if need be, deep-fry in several batches. If you don't have a cooking thermometer, check the oil as it heats by dipping the handle of a wooden spoon into it, when bubbles form around the spoon, the oil is hot enough.

dressing Add just enough dressing to coat the leaves or vegetables in a salad.

pan-frying If the pan starts to get too hot and the food is cooking too quickly, lift the pan up and swirl it gently above the flame or element until it cools down a little.

peeling tomatoes Cut a cross in the base of tomatoes, drop into boiling water for about 10 seconds until the skin starts to peel away at the cross, refresh in iced water then peel.

resting time It is essential that a piece of meat, fish or poultry is set aside to 'rest' after it comes out of the oven or the pan, covered loosely with foil. This allows the juices that have been drawn to the surface by the heat of cooking, to seep back towards the centre so that it is moist throughout and juices don't run all over the plate when it's cut. You must rest meat for a minimum of 20 minutes for a 1 kg piece, or 30 minutes for a larger piece, but you can happily leave it to rest for longer, even an hour or more. When you're ready to serve the meat, return it to the oven at about 200°C for 3–10 minutes until it's warmed through (specific times and temperatures are given in each recipe). Remember that food usually tastes better served warm, rather than piping hot.

roasting meat Roasting is one of the easiest and tastiest ways to cook meat: once it's in the oven you can set a timer and forget about it for an hour or more, plus it can be cooked well ahead of time then put back into the oven to warm through just before serving. So it's worth learning how to do it right. The best way to tell when any meat is cooked is to use a meat thermometer to check the internal temperature. Unless you're a very experienced cook you can't tell by looking at it or prodding it with your finger, and you can't rely on a specific timing as each cut of meat is different and every oven is different. The cooking time will also depend on how long the meat has been out of the fridge before it goes into the oven. The core temperatures of beef and lamb for different degrees of doneness are: 55°C for rare; 62°C for medium; and 70°C for well done. But it's not quite that simple, as the internal temperature of a large piece of meat will keep rising by 6–8°C in the residual heat once you remove it from the oven. So the trick is to take it out when it's still a few degrees below the desired temperature; for medium beef, for example, remove the meat from the oven at about 55°C. If meat has been slow-roasting (over 3–4 hours) at a lower temperature, its core temperature will only increase about 2°C while it is resting, so wait until the internal temperature is a bit higher.

taste Taste at every stage of the cooking, especially before adding salt and pepper, then taste again after seasoning to be sure you've added enough. Season well, and don't be afraid of salt – it enhances all the other flavours in a dish, and most of the salt we consume isn't what we sprinkle on our food or stir into sauces, it's hidden in the over-processed foods we buy. I like to add salt halfway through the cooking, then taste and add more at the end if it's needed.

temperature Bring meat, fish and poultry to room temperature before cooking it, especially if it is being served rare or being cooked for a short time. Don't think food must be served and eaten boiling hot – a lot of food tastes better warm or at room temperature.

toasting nuts Toast nuts in a 160°C oven for a few minutes, turning occasionally, until lightly coloured; watch them closely as they burn easily.

warm plates Always warm serving plates before putting hot food onto them. Some ovens have a special plate-warming compartment, or just soak the plates in hot water for a few minutes, then dry them.

washing vegetables Unless vegetables are being peeled, wash them well under cold water then pat dry. For salad leaves, see the note opposite under salad spinner.

EQUIPMENT

bamboo steamer In Sardinia we'd typically steam in a saucepan, but an easy way is to use an inexpensive bamboo steamer from an Asian grocer. It needs to fit snugly over your largest saucepan or wok so that steam doesn't escape. Wash with soapy water after each use, rinse well and leave in an airy place to dry thoroughly before putting it away.

Japanese mandoline These are fabulous for slicing vegetables wafer-thin for salads. Just remember that they are *very* sharp and always use the guard.

knives You can't cook without a sharp knife, but the good news is you don't need lots of different knives. Start with a chef's knife, which will work well for chopping, slicing and most other jobs, and a small paring knife for jobs such as trimming vegetables. Buy the best you can afford and learn how to keep them sharp with a kitchen steel.

Microplane This is the easiest way to grate citrus zest super-fine – hold the fruit still and pull the grater across the surface of it to get fine shreds of zest without any pith. Microplanes are also handy for grating ginger, nutmeg and hard cheeses.

Mouli This inexpensive piece of equipment is found in every Italian kitchen. It's better than a food processor for making some sauces as it doesn't heat the food up and any skin or pips from the vegetables get left behind in the filter.

potato ricer These look like giant garlic crushers, are inexpensive and essential if you want to make super-light gnocchi as you can push cooked, unpeeled potatoes through them while they're still too hot to handle. The skin gets left behind and the potato ends up in a smooth pile. If you don't have one, peel and mash the potato while it's still as hot as possible.

pots and pans Heavy-based pans are best for even heat distribution. Again, buy the best you can afford and you'll have them for many years.

salad spinner Even if a bag of salad leaves says 'triple washed', don't believe it. Gently toss all salad leaves in a sink of cold water, then lift them out and spin dry in a salad spinner.

thermometers Cooking thermometers are essential for some recipes (such as desserts) and handy for others (such as when deep-frying). The only way to be certain meat is cooked to your liking is by testing the core temperature with a thermometer.

wheel pastry cutter gives a decorative scalloped edge that is traditional for some pastas and pastries, such as Fried Pastry Loops with Honey (see page 174).

ACKNOWLEDGEMENTS

I have thoroughly enjoyed writing this book. Sardinia is in my blood but I have only been able to write about it thanks to the involvement of so many people.

First and foremost, thank you to my wife Marilyn, who shares my dreams and passions and pushes me to achieve more than I ever thought possible, and to my two wonderful children, Martino and Sofia, who make it all worthwhile.

Thank you to my family, who have always supported me: my mother, Maria, who continues to amaze me with her resilience and love for all of us; my father, Tittino, a true Sardinian – hard-working and proud. And to my siblings, Alessandra, Cristiano and Martino (Martino, I wish you could have seen this book). My parents in-law, Rosalie and Tony Annecchini, and brother-in-law, Marco, have embraced me as their own son since I first arrived from Sardinia.

Writing this book has naturally taken me away from my restaurant at times, so I would sincerely like to thank my dedicated team – one of the best in the industry – for keeping things running so smoothly and professionally. In particular our head chef Daniel Mulligan who, after seven years folding culurzones, is as passionate about Sardinian cooking as I am!

Also sommelier Lara Caraturo, for sharing her expertise in Sardinian wines.

Special thanks to Alex Joslyn, who spent endless hours preparing for our recipe testing, and to Dani Signorini, who re-tested many of the recipes. Thanks also to Roberta's husband, Franz Scheurer, who opened his home for recipe testing, provided great wine matches and ran around sourcing last-minute ingredients. Thanks to Alessio Centrito and Alessandro Pavoni for proofreading the Italian recipe titles.

A dish is only as good as the raw ingredients that go into it, so many thanks to suppliers Anthony Puharich from Vic's Meat, Tarek Choker from Demcos Seafoods, Enrico Pusceddu from Icnussa Fine Foods, and Massimo Scala from Salumi Australia.

In Sardinia, thanks to Anna Cadeddu from Sella e Mosca, Mario and Paolo Careddu, Tore Ono, and Gianmarco Sardi, for their assistance and hospitality while we were researching this book.

Warm thanks to publisher Julie Gibbs for her faith in this project, and to her wonderful team for making the whole process such an enjoyable one – especially editor Alison Cowan, designer Daniel New, production controller Elena Cementon, stylist David Morgan and photographer Anson Smart, who brought such a relaxed vibe to the photo shoot.

Last but not least, thanks to my co-author, Roberta Muir, for her professionalism, passion, attention to detail, persistence and determination to complete this book.

INDEX

First published in the UK in 2013 by:
Jacqui Small LLP
An imprint of Aurum Press
74–77 White Lion Street
London N1 9PF

First published by Penguin Group (Australia), 2012

10 9 8 7 6 5 4 3 2 1

Designed by Daniel New © Penguin Group (Australia)
Photography by Anson Smart, except photos on pages iv and vi–viii, which were taken by Franz Scheurer
Styling by David Morgan
Map by Arielle Gamble
Typeset in Alright Sans and Livory by Post Pre-press Group, Brisbane, Queensland
Colour reproduction by Splitting Image, Clayton, Victoria
Printed and bound in China by 1010 Printing International Ltd

ISBN 9781909342101

A catalogue record for this book is available from the British Library.

Strait of Bonifacio

Costa Smeralda

GALLURA

OLBIA-
TEMPIO

Azachena

Rome
250 kilometres

Sennori

Sassari

Tempio
Pausania

Olbia

Oschiri

Padru

San
Teodoro

Sotga

SASSARI

Alghero

Bosa

NUORO

Nuoro

Oliena

Tyrrhenian Sea

Cuglieri

ORISTANO

Oristano

OGLIASTRA

Jerzu

MEDIO
CAMPIDANO

CAGLIARI

Sanluri

Serdiana

CARBONIA-
IGLESIAS

Carloforte

SAN PIETRO

Cagliari

SANT'
ANTIOCO

Mediterranean Sea